Treasures of the Sea
A Novel

By

C. M. Nakken

Chapter 1

◆

It was around 11:30 pm, almost the beginning of a new day. I was preparing, getting ready, getting focused for the task at hand. I have been watching the movements of Gil and Mary Deutsch for three days and three nights. Mary had arrived home that night around 9 o'clock in her red Mercedes. She returned from her book club. Under her arm I could see with my binoculars they had been reading and discussing the book, "Waiting" by Ha Jin. I chuckled to myself for I had read the book. How apropos, in the book the doctor and the woman he loves must wait nearly two decades to consummate their relationship and tonight, I would be consummating my relationship with Gil and Mary but in a different way - - if you viewed murder as an act of intimacy.

Gil had spent the night trimming the roses and surfing the internet, looking and researching cities he and Mary might want to travel to, for they both loved to travel. Gil and Mary were now upstairs getting ready for bed. Gil tried to be in bed by 9:30, read for a bit, watched the 10 o'clock news and the monologue of the Tonight Show. Mary the same, but she would almost always be sound asleep by the time the news was over. Gil and Mary, in the three days I'd been watching them, had made love once and seemed to genuinely care about each other, something I had felt about them when I had met them on the cruise. At least they would be leaving this world together.

I was hoping it would not have to be too painful. I hated it when the husband would hold out, making me torture their wives and them before telling me where I would find the bounty I was looking for.

I was enjoying the comfortable drop of the temperature as happens in the high desert at twilight. For the past three days, I had resided in a small hole on the side of the hill under a camouflage concealment tarp I had hand painted to match the special terrain of this area. During the day, it had been very warm. But I was used to this type of warmth from my military days in the deserts of Kuwait after Desert Storm. During days and nights, I kept going over details, scenarios that might take place and my options. I knew the security system, and even though Gil thought it was high tech when we had talked about it on the ship, I knew it would take me about five minutes to have it totally disarmed in a way that would not alarm the security company. People almost always overestimated their security systems. It offered them comfort. But as Gil researched cities to travel to, I researched security systems and their flaws.

I did my research at the public library using their internet service. I left no personal digital footprint, in fact, even though I was a computer expert, I owned no computer. The world was changing and sometimes it's best to stay hidden in the old world. The old world often gave one a good viewing platform to study and learn about the changes taking place. I loved using the computer, but to have my own meant leaving ghostly shadows about who I was, and personally, I lived my life like a shadow at mid-night on a new moon.

I put on my Tyvek protective suit; it offers the best protection against leaving any DNA and allowed me protection if things got messy and bloody. Bullet holes and blood always leave their mark. I put on shoes two sizes larger than I normally wear, knowing the sands of the desert would make it impossible to not leave footprints. In less than fifteen minutes, I had cleaned up my tiny encampment, exited my perch and was standing inside the house.

Mary had beautiful taste. Their paintings most were exquisite and probably worth quite a bit but not what you could get rid of easily. If this was a simple robbery, these types of things may have been snatched up, but when lives are also to be taken, one must look for different types of plunder. Plunder that leaves little or no trace -- diamonds, cash, gold and silver. Which Gil, through his bragging, had told me they had plenty of.

Card games, a cigar with a nice glass of scotch or in an exquisite gourmet meal on high-end cruises were good ways to get to know a certain type of rich, often new money. I always love the ones that needed to flaunt their wealth. The ones that love to drop names and destinations of where they'd been and loved to tell stories of how they'd accumulated their monies, and particularly I relished it and would pay special attention if they talked about mistrusting the government and banks. A few well-placed congratulations mixed with some adornment about their business skills and agreement about the dangers a big government and many would spend time with me, allowing me to stroke their egos. I was surprised at how easy it was to get into conversations and hints about how I kept a nice nest of money at home, and often they would chime in how they did the same. I found out many men need to keep a portion of the wealth near them to help them feel secure and remind them of their success. Almost always by the end of the 16 to 20-day cruise, I would have as much information as I needed to plan three or four robberies. From there, I would choose the top one or two and start my planning in earnest.

Gil and Mary have been my second pick. They were both in their early 70s. Gil was a blue-collar man who'd worked his way up in the trucking and moving business to own his own company. He and Mary franchised it and sold it to a conglomeration that could take it to the next level, for tens of millions. He was proud of what he had accomplished but didn't give Mary as much credit as she deserved. She had been the one to push them into franchising that Gil would reluctantly acknowledge. She had a cute, fun way of putting him in his place when he got bragging too much. She would just reach over and patted his large tummy and say, "Gil's been very successful, maybe a little bit too much." Everyone would always laugh, and Gil would get the message that his bragging was getting out of line. But he, like many old men love to relive his achievements. Mary didn't brag; she wore her and Gil's accomplishments. If you wanted to know who the top designers were, you had only to look at Mary's wardrobe, and the thing I loved best, Mary loved to wear shiny things, things made from and of gold and diamonds.

A short two and a half hours after entering their home, I was leaving it with my plunder. Gil had given up the combinations to their two safes almost as soon as I had out my cream brulée torch and ripped the front of his wife's nightgown open. I had given him a choice the combination to the safes or the torch to his wife's breasts and then his genitals. I was glad when Gil had chosen wisely, and because of that, I would make his death painless or at least quick. They had both been zip-tied around their ankles and wrists after I had used my Taser to subdue any resistance.

After I had gathered what I came for, I went back to Gil and Mary lying in their large king-sized bed. I zapped each with my Taser again, watched their bodies dance then go limp. I then put my HK VP9 9mm with suppressor to their temples and left two bullets in each of their skulls. I then took off the zip ties, positioned them, and placed a mint on Mary's pillow. I had never taken off the mask I was wearing. Gil and Mary did not need to know the mistake they had made getting too friendly with someone on their Mediterranean cruise. They could go to their death with the beautiful memories of their travels even though I'm sure that was not on their mind when the bullets passed through their skulls and into their designer pillows.

I went to the cheap little mom and pop motel owned and run by an Indian couple originally from New Delhi. It was where I rented a room for a week paying only cash. Within an hour, the gun and Taser I had used was dismantled, the rubber suit and shoes all packed away in a small plastic bag ready for disposal. After a couple more hours, diamonds and precious gems had been taken off the necklaces and the gold or platinum they had been mounted in and the metal was melted down. Gil had 383 golden eagles and 35 pounds of silver in 5-pound ingots and $211,000 in cash in one safe. The other safe had kept Mary's substantial jewelry collection. I estimated its value in just diamonds and the precious metal mountings alone to be around 1 million to one and half million dollars. I loved people who needed to show off their wealth; it allowed me to have an extremely comfortable lifestyle. And Mary sure liked her diamonds.

By the next morning, I was heading west out of Flagstaff on Interstate 40 towards Kingsman here, I caught state Highway 93 and headed north to Nevada, then took different roads up to Northern Nevada. At two places, I stopped and buried parts of the broken-down gun in the desert. Though the gun would be untraceable, it still would be best to leave parts of it strewn in different places. The cash was bundled and packed away in the false bottom in the trunk of my car, as was the gold and silver and the false bottom was soldered shut. Nothing would be found if a search was done, unless the whole car was torn apart and no reason for that would be given. Cruise control was always set at local speed limits for the entire trip.

The diamonds were already in two small boxes between layers of cotton and placed in two prepaid mailing envelopes ready to be dropped in different mailboxes and mailed back to my secure post office box near Hayden Lake, Idaho. I'd chosen to live in this area of Idaho for it was the part of the country where neighbors would leave you alone, ask little questions for they wanted little questions asked. It is a part of the country where people would go to get lost and not be found. I wasn't lost, but I preferred not to be found.

I stopped at a popular camping site, bought some fire-wood and made a fire to cook some coffee, breakfast and burn up my clothes and disposable suit. I picked the site most likely to be used again later that day in left unburnt firewood, making it even more popular. Even though I burned everything up, I wanted other people burning and leaving their garbage mixed in with mine.

It had been a good hunt. I liked my lifestyle, I like the money it brought me, but I'd also come to love seeing the fear in their eyes and the despair when they realized what their fate would be. Often there just be a tear, a single tear running down their face. This was the case with Gil; out of kindness and my respect for him, for he was a decent man, I killed Mary first. I knew he would have wanted it that way.

Chapter 2

◆

Detective Collins had just sat down to his desk when the phone rang. "Bobby, it's just come across the wire. There's another murder outside Flagstaff that fits the description of the one we're working on. An older couple, a Gil and Mary Deutsch, both had been shot in the head twice, marks showed that a Taser was used to subdue them and a mint was left on the pillow of the wife, sound familiar?"

The details of the crime were nearly identical to one that Detective Bobby Collins was working on, another older couple murdered, a Marvin and Mary Renee Bonan, living in Scottsdale, Arizona. A wealthy couple robbed and murdered in their own home three months ago. No traces, no evidence was found, something that's very rare. There were a couple of marks on the security system where clamps had been used to bypass the system. That was the only evidence. The similarities were too profound, two older white couples in their 70s, both very wealthy, robbed with no evidence left behind, Tasers used to disable them, both then made to lay on their beds and killed with two shots to their temples and the mint placed on the pillow of the wife. It had to be the same killer. And It was clear he was a pro and a dam good one.

Detective Bobby Collins had been on the Phoenix police force for 22 years. He was a crusty old cop. Bobby was a recovering alcoholic who'd nearly lost his family to his drinking 2 1/2 years ago. His near ex-wife and son were finally talking to him again after two years of sobriety. They had, to Bobby's surprise, come to the meeting the night he got his 2-year coin. His wife actually sat next to him, but she wouldn't hold his hand or give him a hug. His son gladly did both.

It had been recorded as an "accidental" discharge of his weapon, but he was drunk, scared and angry, a dangerous combination. It was an "accidental" discharge of five slugs into the carpeted floor of their home. Kay moved out that same night with Joe, their five-year-old son. The department forced him to go to treatment or be dismissed. Secretly, he was glad the things had come to a head, but he was now the brunt of every joke with anything to do with flooring. The latest one involved Home Depot. The company had put out an ad saying they were having "killer prices" on new carpet. A copy was placed in the duty room with someone having written over it, "Must've been the work of carpet killer Detective Bobby Collins." He knew the ribbing would never end and rightfully so. It was a crazy way his fellow cops let him know they were glad he was sober. They had been quiet during his drinking days.

He had been secretly glad that his wife, Kay, had taken their son Joseph, whom everyone called JC, and left. It had been the right thing to do. He wasn't sure why she'd never divorced him, but he thought little about it. He was just glad they were at least still legally married. To him, it was one small miracle of recovery; to Kay, it was because she still deeply loved him. Al-Anon had taught her that Bobby was a good man with a terrible illness, not a terrible man with a drinking problem like her mother and others had tried to convince her. She had started Al-Anon two years before Bobby had the incident in their home. After Bobby had shot up the carpet, Kay's first call was to Bobby's Captain, her second call was to her Al-Anon sponsor.

"You want me to call Flagstaff and ask them to keep the crime scene intact, so you and me can head-up for a look-see? They discovered the bodies a couple of hours ago." The person asking the question was Detective Alex Hollander, Bobby's partner for nearly 12 years.

"Yeah, call and tell them we'll be getting in the car with sirens on and we'll be there in three hours. Tell them not to move anything. Tell them we may have a serial killer on our hands." A serial killer is defined by someone who has killed three or more people and with adding this new couple, the killer had entered that special category. It also was a term that always got the attention of any homicide department, so it was not used lightly.

"You okay with that call?" Bobby asked his partner

"Yeah, the damn mints on the pillow did it for me."

They stopped at Captain Colleen Donahue's desk, informed her of what was happening and were on their way to Flagstaff within ten minutes. Alex drove; he enjoyed the speed and the sounds of the siren as they zipped up Interstate 17. He made the drive in two hours forty-five minutes, not a bad time, he'd done it once twenty minutes less, but it had been at night, with a full moon providing good light and almost no traffic. Detective Collins stared out the window locked in a trance wondering about what type of person was into laying out and killing elderly couples. When an elderly person was murdered, it was often murder-suicide, one of them wanting to end it, maybe they had been told they or their partner been diagnosed with an ugly terminal illness or dementia or Alzheimer's or them tired of the pains of being old. Sometimes it was a relative wanting their inheritance a bit early.

But this time, the murders came after a burglary, with the murders being unnecessary. Robberies of the elderly were not that hard; they rarely fought back, so put a mask on and rob them and leave, why lay them out in their bed blankets covering them to make it look like there were sleeping and then two shots to the temples? Why place them in their beds, execute them, and then leave a dam mint on the pillow? Detective Collins had been doing this long enough now that a person, he wasn't ready to rule out a woman, a woman may prey on elderly for the elderly are always easier to control, but he also knew it was most likely a man, a lone man, who had reasons for everything he did. To a killer like him, a serial killer, his killings were like a symphony he had written. With everything he did being a note in his sick symphony, having meaning and bringing him pleasure in some way. Not any real evidence, just clues, the dam mint, it was a challenge, see if you can hear the song I am playing.

Bobby was nervous and scared. Since he gotten sober, he had feelings again and he now listened to them. His fear was telling him that if what he suspected was true, he was up against a serial killer, the likes of which he'd never dealt with before. If the crime scene in Flagstaff was anything like the one in Phoenix, the only thing to be found would be the challenge.

Chapter 3

◆

Alex and Bobby drove directly to the house of the Deutschs, thanks to GPS. The crime scene tape surrounded the house and blue light still flashed, bouncing off the vegetation. They hooked up with Detective Ramirez, the detective Alex had talked to on the phone. "You made good time," he said as he shook Alex's and Bobby's hands.

"I've done better actually by 20 minutes about a year ago. What have we got here?" Alex said proudly.

They all started walking into the house and following the path the detectives had laid out as not to disrupt the crime scene. Detective Ramirez filled them in on what they knew, which wasn't much. "Two dead, the son found them, he was stopping by to pick up his father to go out to breakfast, something they did each day. Instead of Dad being ready and waiting, which would have been the norm, there was no answer when he rang the bell. He used his key to let himself in and found them like this."

By now, they were in the bedroom of the Deutschs. They looked peaceful except for the bullet holes in their temples and the bloodstained pillows. The shooter had shot downward, so the part of their skull that was blown away would be in the back of the head resting on the pillow allowing the Deutschs to somewhat appear as if they were just sleeping. The direction of the shots was identical to those Marvin and Mary Renee Bonan had received from their killer. Detective Collins thought to himself, "It looks like he knows that one of the children would be finding the bodies and wanted it to be less painful. Meaning that he had to be watching and learning routines." Bobby said to Detective Ramirez, "Can

11

you have your men do a 1000-yard perimeter search in all directions think he had to know that the son would find the bodies, which means he had to be watching."

Detective Ramirez moaned, "This 1000-yard perimeter shit, it's going to mean overtime! But okay!" With the death of Marvin and Mary Renee Bonan, they had only done a standard 500-yard perimeter search. Detective Collin made a mental note to himself to go back to the first scene and do a 1000-yard perimeter search.

Bobby was also wondering if the killer had military training, thinking he was in his thirties; check the marks, see if same taser or different one was used, same with the bullets, random thoughts running through his head, but he had learned to pay attention to them. He asked Detective Ramirez to have his men take pictures of the bedroom so he could visually re-create it in his office. In his mind, he wanted and would need to know every detail. He wanted to walk through the room and see it just by closing his eyes; there must be more clues.

The bedroom was the stage where the killer's concert was being played, and somewhere in the bedroom, there most likely were more clues, more notes. This type of killer loved the challenge, loved the taunting of the police with how smart he was almost as much as he loved the killing. Detective Collins was starting to hate and admire the killer. He was good and very thorough, but he also had to be smug and arrogant, believing he was uncatchable. This was a part that Collins hated. Why kill two couples not that many miles apart that had to be part of the taunting, part of his arrogance.

The longer Bobby was in recovery, the more similarities he was seeing between some of the killers he hunted and his own struggles with addiction. The similarity between their world and his drinking was that it was all based on a belief there would never be a day of reckoning. Arrogance and ego were the strengths of his addiction and also the downfall of his addiction. He could sense the same arrogance and the inflated ego of this killer Bobby hoped it would be his downfall too. But Bobby knew some alcoholics never got sober and some killers never got caught. If they were going to catch him, it would be because of good police work, long hours, detailed research, and some old fashion luck.

As he and Alex investigated the bodies more closely, he noticed that Mary's nightgown was ripped in the front. Both Gil and Mary had zip tie marks on their wrist. "More similarities between the two murders it was almost for sure that it was the same killer. Get some measurements and maker of the zip ties used to bind them. I want to compare them and see if they are the same type and maker. It would help confirm our suspicions beyond any doubt." The photographer took detailed pictures of the imprints left by the zip ties and all aspects of the crime scene. Bobby asked to have them put on a flash drive so he could take it back down to Phoenix; it would be quicker than having them sent down. "How about we just skip one level of bureaucratic bullshit today, we've got a serious player we're dealing with."

Detective Ramirez agreed and when his forensic guy objected, "Eric, for Christ sake, just do it, no damn red tape on this one, we got a serial killer."

Bobby cynically threw Eric a flash drive. "Here, put it on this. Our department will pick up the cost."

Bobby and Alex went to the kitchen to talk with the son, Daniel. The detectives had put him in the kitchen for it was clear that nothing had taken place in that room thus, no evidence would be disturbed. He was sitting in shock, his head in his hands as Bobby and Alex entered. Alex started, "We are truly sorry for your loss, we know this is a horrible time, but if you don't mind, can we ask you a few questions?"

Bobby interrupted Alex, "Daniel, first again, we are truly sorry for your loss. Is or anybody we can call who can come be with you. You shouldn't be alone at a time like this." Alex smiled to himself for he'd seen changes, small changes like this, a softening in the crusty old detective's shell ever since treatment.

Daniel told them he had called his wife. She was on the way over but needed to find someone to stay with the kids. Alex went back to the questioning. "I'm assuming your folks have resources. Have you checked to see if anything of value is missing part of us believes this was not just a murder but also a robbery?" Daniel told them it didn't look as if anything was missing. "Do your folks have a safe?"

"Yes, they have two, one in his office and another up in their bedroom for mom's jewelry."

"Do you know the combinations, and if you do, can we have you check to see if anything is missing?" Daniel walked with them to the safe in the office.

"We, didn't have any secrets, the three of us worked next to each other building the company for years, Dad and mother knows where my safe is and its combination, and, I've always known where their safes are and the combinations."

The four of them were standing in front of the safe. Detective Ramirez asked, "Daniel, we're going to need you to put on gloves in case there is any evidence we want to preserve everything we can." The having to put on gloves made the reality hit home; this wasn't his parents' home anymore. It was a crime scene.

Daniel broke down, crying, "Why, why would anybody do this to my mom and Dad?"

Detective Collins put his hand on Daniel's shoulder. "Again, sorry, there are some really horrible people out there, Daniel. This wasn't your parents' fault." Then Detective Collins said something he should never say, "We'll get this son of a bitch, I guarantee you, we'll get this son of a bitch." Detective Collins could feel his own ego, his own emotions slipping into the case it was becoming personal. But he had broken the cardinal rule, never promise the family something you may not be able to give them, and there was never any guarantee the killer would be caught, especially with his talents, this statement had been pure ego.

14

After a bit Daniel collected himself, he opened the safe and found it empty. "Oh my God, everything's gone. Dad kept gold and silver and a lot of cash in here; part of him didn't trust banks and government."

The three detectives and Daniel then went back to the bedroom. Daniel stopped and looked at the bed. There was a sheet covering the bodies, but the outline of his parents were clearly visible. "They were good parents." More tears came to his eyes.

After a bit, Detective Collins softly said, "Daniel, the safe." Behind a picture on the wall next to their bed was a smaller safe, Daniel opened it and they found it too was empty. "We're assuming that your mother's jewelry had been in here and that it was worth quite a bit, is that true."

"Yes, Mom loved jewelry and Dad love to indulge her."

"Do you know if her jewelry was insured?"

"Yes, I know it was, I paid the premium just two weeks ago for that is part of my responsibility at work."

"Good, very good, will need to get the name of the company and the policy number from you." The insurance company most likely has pictures of all the jewelry and we can quickly get pictures and descriptions out to pawnshops. We can check with our sources to see if any jewelry of this magnitude is making its way to the streets."

Daniel said he would get them the name of the insurance company quickly. He needed something to do. He felt so helpless having a task helped alleviate the small bit of misery.

An officer came up to them to let them know that Daniel's wife Maggie had arrived and they all went back to the kitchen. Upon seeing her, Daniel completely broke down, "My God they are dead, they're both dead! Someone murdered Mom and Dad!" Daniel fell into his wife's arms and they cried together. Their closeness was too much for Detective

Collins, it reminded him of how much he had lost due to his alcoholism---his wife. He left the room, telling Alex he would go check on something.

Since treatment, Detective Collins was experiencing lots of emotions. There were still times he didn't know what to do with them, this was one of them. So, he walked back to the bedroom and stared at the bodies and used his old standard technique of turning any feeling he didn't know what to do with into anger. "You son of a bitch, I will get you!" he whispered to himself. It worked. The tears he had felt welling up had been transformed into hatred and super focused attention.

When he was again safely resting in his anger, he walked back into the kitchen speaking to Maggie, "Excuse me, your mother-in-law's nightgown was ripped. She seems like a very proper lady. Would she have worn something in that condition?"

Maggie spoke up, "God no, she would've immediately fixed it or thrown it away. Mary was very proper about her appearance that's totally unlike her. Why? Does it mean something?" Bobby told her he wasn't sure, maybe was something that had been done during the robbery.

"Why would somebody do this to them?" Maggie asked.

"I don't know, ma'am; I just don't know. But thank you, that's helpful to know."

Then Maggie let out a gasp, "He didn't do anything to her, you know, do anything to her, did he?"

Detective Collins felt a bit of relief. He could offer a small bit of good news that images of their loved one being sexually violated wouldn't be added to their minds and memories. "No ma'am, it doesn't look like she was violated in any way." He then thought to himself, "Well, that's not quite true, murder is a violation, of pretty dam big one at that. But I guess it's best not to say something like that." He made a mental note to have the lab checked the gown for DNA where the killer would've had to grab

16

it to rip it, but he was already sure that none would be found. He knew the person they were dealing with was too smart for that.

Before Detective Collins and Hollander headed back to Phoenix, they went out to coffee with Detective Ramirez. The three talked about every detail of what they had seen, looking to see if any of them had any detail that the others didn't. Detective Collins was impressed with Ramirez and the way he put things together. He had called the insurance company and pictures of the jewelry were being faxed over as they had coffee. Ramirez was smart and efficient two good qualities. By the time they were done with coffee, all three of the men were totally convinced that the person who had killed the Deutschs was also the same person who had killed the Bonans. They were also sure that it had been a man even though they didn't have proof. It was time to check the databanks for other murders that would fit the description to see what type of serial killer they may be dealing with.

Chapter 4

◆

By the time I got back to my house in Hayden Lake, the precious gems had arrived at my P.O. Box in Coeur d'Alene, Idaho. I now had time to sort through them and look at them under magnification to see if there any serial numbers had been etched in any of the diamonds or other stones. Only one of the pieces had stones that were traceable in this way. These stones would be tossed into Hayden Lake but not from shore where they may be accidentally found, but into the center part of the lake when I went fishing for my supper tomorrow afternoon.

I was furious with myself; I had broken one of my cardinal rules. I had murdered two couples in the same state within a short amount of time and used the same MO sloppy, very sloppy, not like me. Most likely, because of the distance between the murders, about 150 miles, they would not be put together, but now with computers, I couldn't assume that. I had to assume the connections would be made. I made myself a promise no more killings in Arizona, or if I did, the crime scenes would have to be totally different. No tasers, no mints, maybe death by knife instead of a gun, and a lot of evidence but none connected to me. But nothing in Arizona for a couple of years that would be best.

When I was done checking and sorting all the diamonds and other precious stones, I took the silver bullion melted and recast them into 5-pound bars with no serial numbers on them, at least any that were traceable. I had my own made-up foundry name, "The Teller City Foundry," and numbers embedded in the cast, making them look authentic. Teller city with an old boom and bust mining town in Colorado. It had its glory when Madore Cushman ("Old Crush") had discovered silver in Jack Creek. In 1882 the town was bustling, but by 1885 it was deserted a ghost town. I had run into the ghost town, went out hiking and fell in love with its story, thus "The Teller City Foundry." But if anyone were going to check or try to trace the bullion, it would lead them nowhere.

It was time for a drive. I put the jewels and most of the cash into one briefcase and the gold coins in another and the silver bars in two more. I drove over to Pasco, Washington and the First Federal Savings and Loan showed them my driver's license, the one where the name matched the safety deposit boxes and went in and deposited the precious stones and cash into one of my three large boxes.

I weighed my stones 7.90 ozs of high-quality diamonds, 4.2 ozs of rubies and 1.72 ozs of sapphires. Plus, I also had $3 million in cash. I then drove down to Pendelton, Oregon and the Community Bank and Trust of Pendelton rented a new box and deposited the gold coins and the melted gold from the jewelry that I had turned into a small ingot. And then one more stop in Walla Walla Washington at a personal storage unit I had rented and paid ahead for 15 years with cash. Here I left the silver and the gold in the false bottoms of some dressers and other furniture that, if somebody tried to move, it would be impossible because of the weight—time to go home. I had totaled up as I always did the present value of everything I had was right around eight and a half to eleven million dollars depending on what I could get for the untraceable stones in another country. I knew it was time to stop, but I also knew that it wouldn't be happening. It'd been time to stop long before, I enjoyed it too much, and it was now time to hunt again. There was something addictive about playing God with people's lives in getting paid well for it.

I had a hard time knowing which part of my life I enjoyed the most, hunting of my prey or the pursuing, catching and plundering. I think what I liked most was the challenge embedded in all parts. Could I pick the right people, be convincing enough to get the information I needed? Could I learn their habits enough to find the perfect time, then robbed them and take their lives without getting caught. So far to the 12 couples that now or soon would lay in graves, the answer was-- yes. But I had gotten sloppy and had broken one of my rules. Why? The danger with what I did was that it could be like a string of dominoes. If one falls, they may all fall. I'd left a Domino swinging back and forth. Why? The only answer I could give myself was arrogance, the same reason I always left a mint on the pillow. One clue was okay, but two murders to connect together wasn't. The police dealt with the murder in one way, but if they felt they had a serial killer, they would go crazy, they always took that as a serious challenge.

I knew the prisons were full of stupid, arrogant people, never believing or never caring if they got caught. My mistake was of the first kind believing I couldn't be caught. How stupid of me! I knew if I was caught, I would never go quietly, the way my house and lands were wired with explosives proved that. It was stupid of me to underestimate those chasing me, arrogance is a sloppiness I could ill afford. I despised it in others. It was one reason I killed these couples most were arrogant about their wealth. Now I was showing the same characteristics I despise so greatly in others. As a fellow hunter had once told me, "Watch out what you hunt. If you do it well, you start to become like that which you hunt. As you know, its habits and its attitudes, they can swallow you up." He loved the quote, "If you stare into the abyss know that the abyss is staring into you." Was the arrogance of my victims rubbing off on me?

I needed to find out if a connection between the murders was being made.

I drove down to Flagstaff to see what was happening with the crime scene. It was a week and a half after the murder that took place high on the hill about a mile from the Deutschs' home and observed what was happening. I soon had my answer. Though there was only one policeman still stationed at the site. I noticed that they had searched the parameter 1000 yards out. By doing this, they had found where I had been hiding for three days watching the Deutschs. There was yellow police tape around the trench where I had been observing Gil and Mary from. This was not the standard perimeter search protocol 500 yards search. Whoever was working the case was not dumb. I drove down to Phoenix and the crime scene there and noticed that they had extended their parameter search from 500 to 1000 yards and it also found where I had been hiding

20

watching and studying the Bonans. Even though they had found where I have been watching from, I knew they would find no biological evidence only confusing trash I had left just for that purpose. When covering your tracks, it's always helpful to have a bag of random trash to be scattered. But that they had moved the search from 500 yards to a thousand at both crime scenes means they had made the connection between the two. "Damn, you fool you keep thinking they're not as smart as you what happens the day you meet a detective who is, prison or death no more play, you fool." I was mad, mad at myself. This was not just a mistake; it was opening the door a crack into my world, a world where I wanted no one but myself inside.

It was not a pleasant drive back to Hayden Lake. I had lots to think about, lots to chew myself out for, lots to sort through. Why had I broken my own rules? Who was the detective who decided to extend the search area? I needed to know who I was up against. Had I left any other clues? Were there other ways I had gotten sloppy? Over and over in my head, I relived my three days of watching and the nights of my intimate encounters with the Deutschs and the Bonans.

I got into my boat to go fishing and to think. Also, part of me wanted to relive this last hunt it had been so delicious they were so afraid when I brought them to their bedroom. I could tell they thought they would be dying. They watched me in fear, they watched each other in sorrow. Because their mouths were gagged, they tried to say goodbye to each other with their eyes. Mary was the first to tear up and cry soon Gil had a tear running down his face there was a longing in his eyes wishing he could get back to the life they had just hours ago, but that life was gone. I would make sure of it.

Part of me especially enjoyed it when I would run into a couple like Gil and Mary. They were less arrogant than the others. But, they truly loved each other. Love had not worked out well for me and part of me hated the concept. They probably would've given up the money and jewels just for more time with each other. But that would not be the case. The kindest thing I could do was to make it quick. I put the gun to Mary's head. It had a silencer specially made for me by a man in Canada. He had made all of my guns; none traceable, all of them deadly.

I put two bullets in Mary's head then walked over to Gil, who was going insane with what he had just witnessed. I put the barrel a couple of inches away from his temple and popped off two more rounds I didn't have to watch their sadness anymore I just had to watch their designer pillows turn red, crimson red. I took the gags off their mouths and put them into the plastic bag. They would be taken with me. I arranged the two as if they looked as if they were having a restful night except for the crimson red pillows I then put a mint on Mary's pillow. "Sleep well, fellow voyagers, sleep well!" I went around the bedroom looking for any clues I may have left; there were none to be found.

I then slid out of the house like a soft summer breeze leaving no trace except for maybe a couple of shoe prints of an extra-large shoe there would soon be disposed of in a barrel of acid. The vehicle I had bought under a false name with a false ID was tucked away in a small grove in Northern Pines about a mile and half from the Deutschs' home. I changed clothes putting everything into the plastic bag that would go into the barrel of acid tucked away in an old silver mine just off of HWY-140 in northern Nevada. I had bought the land with the old silver mine tucked away on it before my first hunt. It had a single purpose. I always felt peaceful when spending time within the mine it was quiet so very quiet. I could hear myself think along with the desert rats that would scurry in and out of the tunnels they never bothered me. I never bothered them. I needed to find out who the detectives were working on the case. That wouldn't be hard, just a phone call or two from a curious citizen. They were either lucky or very smart deciding to move the search out from the standard 500 yards to 1000 yards; the worst-case scenario would be if he or they were both.

A couple of days later, I called the Flagstaff Police Department on one of my burner phones. "I may have a tip about the murders of Gil and Mary Deutsch. Could you please tell me which detective is working on that case and please connect me to them." There was a slight hesitation, probably wondering whether this is a prank call or something that could help the case.

"That would be Detective Ramirez. Let me put you through to him." As I was being transferred, I hung up and picked up another burner phone this time I called the Phoenix Police Department.

"I may have some information is helpful about the murders of Marvin and Mary Renee Bonan can you please tell me which detective is working that case and please connect me to him."

There was no hesitation this time, "That would be Detective Collins and his partner Detective Alex Hollander, I'll transfer you." Again, I hung up. I had my information. Now I just need to find out who they were. This would involve a road trip stopping at some different libraries to use their computers to do some research. I didn't mind the many miles I would be putting on my Subaru Outback, driving allowed me time to think, to review and plan. I always used the cruise control set exactly at the posted speed limit. I knew the gas stations and cafes along my routes that didn't have cameras. I worked to walk and drive through the world casting as little shadow as possible, Mr. Vanilla--there would be plenty of time for personality on the cruise, now was not the time.

I left the outskirts of Hayden Lake, heading west found my entrance to I-90 through Coeur d'Alene and headed to Spokane. My first stop was the Spokane Community College Library over on North Green Street. It was a place I visited often when I wanted to read or use the internet. I knew where all the security cameras were and I knew how to position myself to avoid any direct shots. I always wore my baseball cap for the Spokane Indians, a minor league baseball team based in Spokane. Me and Mary the librarian another Indian's fan exchanged words about the bad season they were having. I gave her my card and she assigned me to one of my favorite public computers, all out of sight from cameras. I typed in the words Detective's Tucson Police Department. It didn't take me too long to find out the information I needed about Detective Ramirez. He was not too new to his profession. He had been a decorated officer making it to the ranks of detective three years ago. Ramon Ramirez had been on the force for 12 years, was a father of three, with two commendations. I found his home address and noted it in case I needed to visit him someday.

Many years ago, I had escaped being caught once by a very clever detective who had a common home accident. He was a known heavy drinker besides being a clever detective and happen to fall down his stairs into his basement where he broke his neck. His BAC (Blood Alcohol Content) was .31 after I made him drink a half a quart of vodka on top of what he had already had that night. The city's department and budget were small. My research told me his cases would be given over to the other detective in their unit. This other detective was a stupid man who couldn't come up with the answer to how much is two and two.

I then typed in detectives of Phoenix Police Department. As I investigated Detective Bobby Collins and Detective Alex Hollander, I felt a small twinge in my chest. They were old-time detectives both had been on the force many years. I read over all the cases I could find in the papers they had been involved in. They were always described as thorough an efficient, especially Detective Collins, the lead dog in their partnership. Both had several commendations in both had worked in the homicide department for over 10 years where Detective Ramirez had only been in homicide a year. Detective Collins also lectured and taught at the Phoenix Police Department Academy. The more I read, the more I realized it was probably Detective Collins who had ordered the search to be expanded. Like with Detective Ramirez before I left the library, I made sure I had the home addresses for the two in case I needed to pay them a surprise visit if they got to close.

Seeing who I was up against, I decided it was not a time for more robberies and murders. It was probably best to switch over to hunting mode. That would take me out of the country for a while so I could watch from a distance and let my contacts inform me if they were putting things together. When you're as successful as I had been in my career, you build up many relationships, people who make part of their livelihood on what you do. Many people benefited from my success and would want to see it continue. It's always easier to disappear into the world when you're already out in the world. Yes, this would be a good time to go hunting for more prey. Time for a long cruise.

Chapter 5

On the way home, I headed over to see Susan Ducati at the Pleasure Time travel agency. I had a long-standing relationship with Susan. She was a lady in her late 30s or early 40s with long blonde hair she kept piled and styled on top of her head, looking very professional. She knew my style of cruising and how I was an avid poker player. She always helped me find cruises that fit my current needs. "Daniel, how nice to see you! You've got the travel bug–I can see it in your eyes."

Actually, what she saw was my desire to hunt again. I laughed. "Does it show that much?"

She nodded and smiled. "Yes, it does, my friend, yes it does." Part of Susan's smile was because she knew there would be a good commission for her because she knew my taste for high-end cruises. At a minimum, I always booked a suite with all the amenities that someone with wealth would get.

"Daniel, where are you thinking?"

I smiled. "Susan, I'm thinking of finally pulling that plug; I'm thinking perhaps Asia we've always talked about it, but what's popular this year?" Susan didn't even answer the second part of the question; she instantly talked about how there were some beautiful new packages for exploring Asia.

"How long are we thinking, Daniel? I know and love that you're not one of those slam-bam thank you, ma'am, seven-day cruisers." I got the sexual innuendo. She was always quite professional but also flirted with me. I could see her excitement, anticipating a sizeable commission on an expensive cruise; I was a good customer for her, and I paid in cash. Something she could never figure out she always thought I was just eccentric, which I was.

"At least a month, maybe up to two." I knew that Susan would focus on showing me cruises of near two months in length or longer; she was a great travel agent, but also predictable looking out for herself and me at the same time and in that order. And I couldn't fault her for looking out for herself. I always did.

"Oh my God, Daniel, Ocean Sails has just listed a new cruise on the Odyssey II, a delightful ship, from San Francisco to Singapore. It's a 58-day voyage from San Francisco to Hawaii, then up to Ketchikan, Alaska; then Anchorage, and then the Aleutians before heading over to Japan, Korea, China, East Timor, Thailand, Fuji–a bunch of places in Asia, wow there's even two days in Ho Chi Minh City Vietnam–and ending up in Singapore where you would fly back from. That's a very good airport and Singapore airlines is one of the best for your flight back home. I think it would be perfect. Is fifty-eight days too much?"

I told her the time seemed just about right. I had traveled on Ocean Sails cruise line often before, and I liked it. Its clientele were mostly high-end wealthy clients but not ostentatious. What I hunted. "Susan, when does it leave?"

She told me it was set to depart about a month and half from now. "That would be perfect; let's start looking at suites." I told her it had been a profitable year–she didn't need to know that meant two couples robbed and murdered. "I wanted to upgrade from the Penthouse Suite that I would usually book. She got a twinkle in her eyes.

"Daniel, have you ever thought about the owner's suite? There is a hell of a lot of perks that come with it, the best one is your own private concierge. They'll treat you like God; you'll get both sunrise and sunset views. Something to think about, especially if you've had a good year. And, it will give you a lot of status with the other passengers." Susan was throwing out the big carrot.

I gave her one of those looks a bit nervous and excited at the same time. "Hell, with it, let's do it!"

We moved to the larger table in her office. We took out a map and went over the trip. She also handed me a sheet with the onboard features that came with the Owner's Suite. "You'll get a personal concierge like I said that's big, all the shore excursions you want, internet, of course, personalized robes and all drinks the best brands come included. Plus, I'm sure I can get you about $15,000 in shipboard credit."

"Oh, that reminds me, Susan, I have a little gift for you." I reached into my briefcase, pulled out a small box and handed it to her.

She opened it and let out a gasp. "Diamond earrings!"

"Yes. I appreciate what you do for me so much, and as my last trip was coming to an end I had about $2000 in unused shipboard credits, and I thought of you–thought you might like some nice earrings." I didn't want to tell her that the last woman who wore them was now dead. If there were some nice diamond earrings with no distinctive detail that kept them untraceable, I would save them to give as gifts. They had opened many doors and legs for me. Ladies do like their diamonds.

She put her hand on mine and told me how beautiful she thought they were. "Daniel, you didn't have to do this! But how thoughtful of you! Oh my God, they're just beautiful."

I had always known she was attracted to me. She got a very seductive look in her eyes. I knew if I had wanted her, she would've gotten on top of her desk and let me take her. But everything was going to be professional, at least on my end, at least for now.

"All I ask is that when you wear them, you think of me and how much I appreciate all your help with my travels." Her hand was still on mine, and she squeezed it tight, letting me again know she would be mine for the taking, but I knew that all she saw in me was money.

I changed the subject. "Which shore excursions would you recommend?"

She put the earrings on and modeled them for me and then went back to being professional, and we went over good places to see. "You're going to have one full day in Hanoi. I could arrange for a private guide if you like; I'm sure that I can get Ocean Sails to throw that in as a reward for being a multi-time customer. There are some fascinating war museums in Hanoi if you like history. The same holds when visiting Saigon, now Ho Chi Minh City, where you spend two days and your concierge might even double as a guide. As we talked, Susan kept making the trip sound on more and more exciting. She was a great saleswoman. By the end, I was indeed looking forward to visiting Asia. I had never been there; Europe, yes; South America, yes; the Middle East, yes; but Asia, never.

"I have to ask, as I've never been on the Odyssey II, but what I've heard is that it's one of Ocean Sail's smaller ships; is there a card room?"

She laughed. "Daniel, I'd never put you on a ship where there wasn't one. I know how much you like a good poker game and I've heard that you're pretty good. One of my other clients was telling me how he had lost a good deal of money to someone on his last trip. I knew you were on the ship, since I had booked you, and as he described the man's demeanor, I knew it was you. I smiled as he ranted on about you; you out-bluffed him good!"

I smiled, listening, acting humble. "If you don't mind, who was the gentleman?"

Susan leaned forward, twisting her new earrings whispering, "I shouldn't say, but it was a long-term client who lives in Flagstaff. I'd met him and his wife when I worked there for a bit decades ago, a Mr. Gil Deutsch."

Susan didn't know it, but she had become a loose end that would need cleaning up. She had sealed her fate when she said, "Mr. Gil Deutsch." I smiled, but inside I was disappointed, thinking to myself, "Damn, Susan! Really! Susan, you've been the best travel agent I've ever had. I'll let you book this next trip, and then I'll need to visit you."

We spend a delightful three hours going over the ship's ports of call, booking side trips and setting up private tours, for I genuinely was interested in exploring the Far East, knowing that someday it may be a place where I go to get lost.

I used the energy that had been in the room earlier to make what I had to do easier. As we were ending, I took Susan's hand, held it gently as I looked into her eyes and said, "Susan, I really appreciate how much you do for me. Every time you help me plan my next adventure; you understand my interests; you're so good at what you do. These times when we get to sit together and plan, I do enjoy my time with you." I smiled as I squeezed her hand a bit, and she squeezed my hand back, staring into my eyes. "Sweet lady, don't be surprised if you go on a nice exciting journey soon."

She looked at me very seductively. I met her glance with a similar one, "You've got something in mind, don't you, Daniel, you little devil? Now I understand that sweet gift of those earrings. I want you to know I'm open to what I believe you want." She leaned over and kissed my cheek.

I kidded back with her acting with a fake shock. "Susan, you, naughty but beautiful girl!"

She squeezed my hand again. "Daniel, you have no idea! You have no idea, but I hope you do someday soon."

I looked down at her body and smiled, "God, I wish I didn't have to go right now, but business calls, and well, that's how I pay for these trips. My business is my true mistress." I knew this would sit well with Susan. She was all about money. She liked me, but she also loved the excellent

30

commissions she was making off me, the diamond earrings and the air of wealth about me, all aphrodisiacs to her. I'm sure she had the fantasy of becoming my girlfriend, maybe even my wife, and having access to my resources. I enjoyed playing with this, and she smiled at me and pushed out her chest even more. I smiled and licked my lips, "Susan, I do believe you're trying to seduce me with your beautiful looks, your sweet smile, that gorgeous body of yours, and damn, it's working."

She smiled gently and seductively, touching her breasts. "Any time, Daniel, any time! My sensitive girls love to be let out and played with."

I bit my lip. "Oh damn, I wish I didn't have to go."

Susan took my hand and led me to the door, "Daniel, you go do your business. I've got to get busy firming up the details for your cruise. I'll be waiting for you, but don't make me wait too long."

As I walked out the door, I shook my head. I was going to miss her talents; she had been the perfect travel agent. She was so good with details, something I always respected. I had things to take care of, so her death would not look like a murder. There would be no similarities that would tie it to the other murders. I was going to make sure of that. She was not the only one who was good with details.

Chapter 6

───────◆───────

Two days later, I got a package in my post box in Coeur d'Alene with everything that I would need for my cruise. I went for a long drive planning out what needed to be done, then got out a burner phone and called Susan, "Susan, It's Daniel here. I got the package, and everything looks perfect, absolutely perfect, thank you!"

"Great, Daniel, great. I don't know if you noticed, but I was able to get you $10,000 in shipboard credits. How are you?" There was a sensual tone to her voice.

"I'm wonderful. I've been thinking about you a lot. I forgot to ask you, do you have a boyfriend?"

"No, Daniel, I don't. It's just my cat and me."

"I hate to have to ask you this again, but can you be discreet, very discreet? It's just the nature of my business."

She laughed. "Oh god, yes, you've never heard me talk about any of my other clients except for Gil, and he was basically giving you a compliment. I only told you because you're special and I know you'll probably not run into him and Mary again on any other cruises. Yes, I can be very discreet. But I can't guarantee about my cat," she said to lighten the mood. She had no idea how true that her statement was; she wouldn't be running into Gil anymore. It was nice to hear that she didn't know about Gil and Mary's murder yet.

"I'm so glad to hear this. I haven't been able to stop thinking about you since the last time we were together." I could almost hear Susan smiling,

"Good, Daniel, I want you thinking about me." Her voice changed, getting softer, more sensual and a bit naughty. "Have you been thinking about my big breasts? I hope so! I'm squeezing them right now thinking about you."

Sounding dumb, naïve and innocent, I said, "Really, you're touching them right now oh my god?" "Yes, Daniel, I am, but I wish it were you who was touching them." I then asked her, "Susan, do you like cocaine?"

She kept her sensual voice. "Daniel, I've only tried it a couple of times, but it was nice. Why are you into it?"
"I've only done it a few times myself, but I hear it greatly intensifies the sexual experience."

"Well, then you'll have to bring some along, won't you. I want to give you the most intense night of your life. I want to ride you like one of those mechanical bulls at a cowboy bar."

"Sounds wonderful and I going to do things to you that nobody has ever done before." The thought ran through my mind, "or ever again."

She laughed loudly. "Then you'll have to get very creative. I've done some crazy kinky things in my life; I'll tell you about them later; or do them with you later."

"Kinky good that's my specialty, Susan, that's my specialty. Remember, my sweet; discretion. Is there a good time to come by tonight?"

"I won't tell a soul that we'll be getting together. Would 5 o'clock work? We could have supper. I'm a pretty good cook."

"I'm sorry that's a little too early. I have a supper meeting with investors. I must attend." But I wanted the sun to be down, fewer chances of being seen.

"How about 8 o'clock? I'll have dessert ready for you, me. Do you like whip cream?" she said with a chuckle.

"That would be perfect, absolutely perfect! And yes, I love whip cream. I'll bring some cherries."

"No need I already have them."

Precisely at 8 o'clock that evening, I was standing at Susan's door. I knew right where she lived, for I had driven by it a few times over the last couple of days. I decided to park two blocks to the south of her house, avoiding the intersection north of Susan's house where there was a traffic camera. Also, a neighbor four doors north of her home had one of those Ring doorbells, which show and can videotape who was at the door. They also record persons walking by on the sidewalk. I was dressed quite informally with my New York Yankees baseball cap pulled down over my forehead. I rang the bell, and as I heard Susan coming to the door, I removed the cap and stood there with the big Cheshire cat grin on my face as she opened the door. It was immediately clear to me that she had been to the hairdresser that day, for her strawberry-blond hair was beautifully layered and styled. The evening was hot, and Susan was in short shorts and wearing a top that showed her lovely cleavage. She was showing off how sexy she could be. She looked great.

"My god you're beautiful, I mean you're always beautiful, but you're especially beautiful! Dam, do you look hot!" I wanted her to feel relaxed, so I was stumbling over my words. "You're so pretty, so very pretty, you got me stammering and stuttering like a schoolboy."

She smiled. "Good, I've always liked you, Daniel, and I want tonight to be especially enjoyable for you. I know it already is for me." I handed her the bottle of wine I have brought; she didn't even notice the super-thin stealth latex gloves I was wearing designed to be almost invisible.

There would be no prints of mine on the bottle; there would just be hers. She invited me in and gave me a big hug pressing her breasts up against me. Then she kissed me. "I hope you don't mind? I've wanted to do that from the day I met you."

I smiled again. "Not a bit, your lips taste like…"

"Strawberries!" she said. "It's a flavored lipstick I got today. I want everything to be special for you."

I thought to myself, "I am going to miss her!"

She brought me into the living room. I asked her where her cat was, and she told me that I'd never see him. "Marcus isn't stranger friendly." She invited me to go sit down in the living room while she went to pour us some wine. I yelled to her in the kitchen, "I brought some of that cocaine I was telling you about, extra pure. Do you mind if I lay some out? I hear it's so good it'll make your brain go dead, and all you'll be wanting is naughty nasty things done to your body."

She chuckled and yelled back, "Absolutely, if that's true then give me an extra big line. I want my body wanting and ready for anything and everything." There was a coaster on the table, and I poured a nice large pile of the drug on to it and using a card I would dispose of later made it into one low fat thick line the size of the straw end. Susan came back into the room, holding two glasses of wine but also topless. "I've always wanted to show you my boobs! I thought maybe you'd like to snort some of that cocaine off my breasts. I would like that would you?"

"Oh my god, Susan, you're more beautiful than I ever dreamed of and so naughty! Absolutely, but first you! I've got everything ready." She gave me a glass of wine. I held it up and toasted, "To journeys and new adventures!"

She repeated the words staring me in the eyes using her sultry voice, "To journeys and new adventures!" I handed her the bag I had taken the drugs from I wanted her fingerprints on it. "Isn't it pretty it's so white and hold so much pleasure?" Susan looked at it smiled and winked at me, then put it down on the table. She picked up the 4-inch straw I had laid next to the coaster, put it in her nose and using her other hand push down on her other nostril. "Inhale as hard and deep as you can sweetie, I want you to get it all, then it will be my turn, and I'll snort a little off each breast, don't want to show favorites."

Susan inhaled hard and deep. I watched most of the powder travel up the straw and into her nose and lungs. Instantly she sat up her eyes wide open, and she gasped for air. Within seconds she fell back on the couch dead, the straw still in her hand. Susan didn't know that it wasn't cocaine she had inhaled into her lungs, but heroin heavily laced with pure fentanyl guaranteed lethal. I was so glad it was quick and painless for her. I did care about her. I poured the rest of my wine into her glass, and when in the kitchen gently lifted the bottle and brought it to the table and put it next to Susan's glass.

I looked around the house to my surprise, her computer was on. I checked her social media, and there was no mention of her having a date she kept her promise to be discreet. I went into her bedroom and put two more small bags, one of heroin laced with the fentanyl and another one of good quality cocaine in her panty drawer. I looked inside her nightstand and smiled. Laying on top was a dildo and another small bag. I'm presuming it was cocaine.

Susan was making my job easy as she had always made my travels. I gently picked up the dildo making sure to pick it up by the end she would insert, for I wanted her fingerprints on the other end if there was an investigation. I brought it to where Susan was and laid it on the couch. The scene was set; it looked as if she was a woman settling into a night, a relaxation and self-pleasuring that had gone terribly wrong. I went over the house twice making sure there was no trace of me before I left. As I was going out the door, I looked over at Susan's lifeless bare-chested body slumped back on the couch. "To journeys and new adventures," I whispered and then shut the door and walk to my car.

The next week I went to the library and brought up the newspaper searching for any stories. Buried in the local section: Susan Ducati, owner of Pleasure Time Travel Agency died of an accidental drug overdose in her home last Thursday night. The article described how shocked her friends were and how well-respected she had been. Her funeral would be that Friday I sent a dozen strawberry-colored roses with no card to the funeral home. I would not be attending the funeral.

Chapter 7

◆

Kay Collins had always been around cops. Her father Joseph, had been one. Joe, as everyone called him, was one of those surly old cops–tough and rugged outside the house; but when he walked in the door, he'd find his wife and plant a big kiss on her. Then find Kay, if she hadn't already run to him, and pick her up so his little princess could wrap her arms around his neck and give him a big bear hug. He was always kind, gentle and understanding with her right until the day he was ambushed and shot while conducting a routine traffic stop.

Joe had stopped a man because his tail light was broken; he was going to give him a warning ticket but when he walked up to the car window, his killer put three slugs into his neck and chest. He had no idea that the man was wanted on a warrant for violating a protection order for domestic abuse. Joe's partner was still in the police car running the plates and swearing at the computer – this happened in the days when the police were starting to add computers to their squad cars – when the shots rang out and he saw Joe fall to the ground. Officer Gary McMure instinctively jumped out of his car to help his partner. McMure had immediately drawn his gun, and thankfully he had, for as soon as he was out of his car, he saw the perpetrator stepping over Joe – who was grabbing his neck trying to stop the bleeding – and coming towards him with a crazed look in his eyes and a gun in his hand. Their confrontation was brief; Officer McMure was a champion marksman and had been a sniper in the Army. The perpetrator had reached the back of his car when one shot rang out, hitting him directly in the middle of his forehead. The gun battle was over.

By the time Gary got to his partner, he was already fading away from the loss of blood. He had just enough energy to whisper out, "Tell Mitten and Margie I love them. I'm sorry. I'm so sorry!" Mitten had been Kay's pet nickname ever since she was a baby and Joe would hold her up with one of his monstrous hands. He told his wife, "She fits perfectly in my hand like a mitten." They both laughed, and the name stuck.

Joe's funeral was one of the largest the state had ever seen. Besides being a police officer, he was also a decorated war hero from Vietnam with a purple heart and a bronze star, earned when the bullet had grazed him as he carried a wounded buddy for more than a half-mile through a firefight with North Vietnamese regulars. There were policemen from every state in the union, even Hawaii; and there were hundreds of Vietnam vets. The man he had saved in Nam, Bob McCarthy, sat next to Kay and her mother at the funeral. When they handed Margie the flag, she immediately turned to Kay. "You have this, Mitten. He'd want you to have it. Give him a big bearhug."

Kay pulled it tight to her chest, and to this day she swears she heard her father whisper, "I love you, Mitten!"

At the funeral, she met Bobby for the first time. He had been one of the officers and detectives chosen to carry her father's casket. Though he was ruggedly handsome, tough, and a bit crusty when he came up to her to offer his condolences, she noticed a tear in the corner of his eye. Margie had seen Kay's immediate attraction to Bobby. After the funeral, she worked behind the scenes to set them up. She didn't care that Bobby was ten years older than her daughter. Kay was 22 and Bobby was 32. Margie had no qualms about her daughter dating a cop; to her, it was the most honorable profession a husband could ever have.

Bobby Collins always kidded Kay he was her father's replacement. They both knew there was some truth in that, but neither of them cared. They dated for a year and quickly decided to get married when Kay became pregnant. When she gave birth, and it was a boy, there was no question what his name would be: Joseph. His grandfather's triangle-shaped flag hung above his grandson's crib in a framed box.

It was a little over a year after Joseph's birth that Bobby's drinking got out of control. The wife of a fellow police officer who lived just down the street called Bobby in hysterics, crying for help. Her husband, with no warning, had hung himself in the garage. Bobby rushed over. Bobby climbed on the chair and cut him down. The only way he seemed able to get that image out of his mind was with bourbon.

Kay had asked Captain Colleen Donahue for help. She had been a long-term family friend. Donahue sent Kay to Al-Anon, telling her she needed to get her head in order and wait for the day when the house of cards of Bobby's drinking would come crashing down.

Colleen's father had been an alcoholic but died sober. That was why Kay called Colleen right after Bobby took out his revolver and placed five shots into their floor. He was shooting at the imagined ghost of the friend he had cut down in that garage. In disgust and panic after the shooting spree, he threw his gun down on the floor. Kay quickly picked it up, put it in the gun safe, slam the door shut and called Colleen. Colleen Donahue was a second cop on the scene; the first was Detective Alex Hollander, Bobby's partner the captain had called him. Captain Colleen Donahue was entering the house as Kay and Joe were leaving it to go to her mothers. Colleen and Alex brought Bobby to detox, and he was placed on a 72-hour hold. The next day Captain Colleen talked to him in her official capacity giving him the ultimatum of treatment or resigning. She ended with, "Please choose treatment. We need good cops, and you're one of the best detectives I've ever seen plus I want my friend back, you, sonofabitch." Bobby chose treatment.

Bobby received treatment at Hazelden in Minnesota. He took to treatment and the 12 steps of Alcoholics Anonymous like a fox to a hen house; he ate up everything he could. The experience not only fed his head but also fed his heart. Helped by a good counselor, Jim Syverson, Bobby put his nightmares behind him. Helped by AA, he put his drinking behind him. He never looked back. But Kay would make sure before allowing him back into the house. She was a mother bear, and she was tired of death. She pledged to herself that she would wait to see if her husband got sober and back to being the good man he was before letting

40

him back in the house. After treatment, the clock started ticking. She had been told in treatment, during family week, that if Bobby stayed sober for two years and worked a solid program most likely, he would be sober for life. That became the marker for her. She wasn't even going to talk about then getting back together until he was two years sober. She made that clear to him. So, she watched him from a distance for two years that didn't matter to Bobby. If she had wanted or needed to wait for ten years, he would've waited; he was sure he had lost her, but she waited. He had forgotten both were the types it only got married once.

Chapter 8

The next days were spend with Bobby and Alex going over every item of evidence looking at the connections trying to hear the song the killer was singing. They were coming up with nothing of substance. Thursday afternoon around 4 o'clock Sandy de Cottle, a young a genius of a researcher with a great love for details came to them excited going crazy bubbling over with excitement about her findings. "Guys, it's confirmed, it's confirmed we've got a well-honed serial killer. There had been three other murders with the same MO, one in Michigan, one in Minnesota and one in Arkansas in all three of them the killer left the mint on the pillow. All were husband-and-wife; all were wealthy and had been burglarized. I know there's more, I know it! But many of the other states aren't connected to the national data bank yet, so I'll have to do a state-by-state search. I'll bet you a steak dinner that there's more."

Alex went over to her and kissed her on the cheek. "Sandy, damn you're good, you've already earned a steak dinner you find any more, I'll upgrade it to steak and lobster."

She smiled. "At Steak 44?" Steak 44 was probably the most exquisite steakhouse in the Scottsdale area of Phoenix.

Bobby smiled. "At Steak 44! If you don't mind the company of a couple of crusty old detectives."

She laughed. "Make the reservations for a week from Friday. I'm going to stay here all night. This guy is pissing me off I've got a pair of grandparents who are just the type this guy would go after and I'd be lost without them, we are going to get this son-of-a-bitch aren't we?"

Both Alex and Bobby enjoyed and admired Sandy. Even though she was only in her late 20s, she was as hard-core as any detective on the force, though she was still a bit naïve in certain areas. But with her skills with a computer, she had put away more criminals than many of the detectives. "Shit with you on his trail we'll get him now get back to your researching and your computer and do whatever you do, I'm hungry for a good steak, and I can already taste those asparagus fries." She left the room as enthusiastically as she had entered it.

Alex watched her perfectly rounded ass as she walked out of the room. He said nothing for he knew that Bobby would've shaken his head and told him to stop being a dirty old man. Alex was sure that Bobby had never looked at another woman since Bobby had first seen Kay. Alex once had made some comment about the pretty ass of some young girl walking down the street and how nice it was, for he was an ass man. He had gotten a half an hour lecture from Bobby about how at their age it was their job to protect the innocence of the young ladies and not to feed off their good looks and how the days of objectifying women needed to be over. Alex kidded him back. "I'm glad to hear that you've burned your bra. I'm not chasing them. I'm just enjoying the scenery." But Alex never won those arguments; he quickly learned to keep those types of thoughts from his partner. Bobby was too decent of a man to listen to any old lecherous comments.

Alex was still caught up in his thoughts about Sandy's ass when Bobby blurted out, "Let's go talk to Colleen I'd like her permission to get the files from the other states, I've got a feeling there's going to be more maybe a lot more. I'd also like to get a conference room assigned we can start posting up all the evidence from all the different murders." Alex followed along, still enjoying his thoughts about Sandy as they walked into the captain's office.

"Captain, Sandy has found three more cases in other states with the same damn MO, and she sure and we are too, that she'll be finding more.

She's going to be looking into the states that aren't yet connected to the national database."

"Shit, guys! Shit, I was wondering what the hell we stumbled into, we've sure stepped into it this time. Why couldn't it have been some other city with a bigger budget than ours." She was clearly more upset than usual. She was throwing out her thoughts into the room. "Fuck! What states?"

Alex piped in, "Arkansas, Minnesota, and Michigan." "Would it be okay if we get a conference room assigned? We want to start laying out all the evidence on the walls. I'm going to send for the files when we get done here."

She answered, "Yeah, of course! God damn serial killers this is going to mean overtime you know that and I know that and we're already stretched thin on our budget. God damn serial killers, God damn overtime!"

Bobby threw in, "And he's good, real good, so it's not going to be easy." Captain Colleen was frustrated by something else, not just this case.

"Fuck! Set up in conference room C, it's the biggest one we've got. Can the two of you handled it, or are you going to need more bodies?"

Looking at Bobby. Alex answered, "For now I think we can handle it, but if it is okay, we'd like to use Sandy a lot more to help research data she's damn good she's the one who found these three other cases."

"Sure, sure, whatever you guys need, within limits though, we're stretched damn thin. "Alex turned to leave, waiting for Bobby to do the same. "I'll catch up with you in a minute Alex. I want to talk to the Cap. about something."

As Alex left the room, Bobby sat down. "Okay, Cap. What's going on? You're clearly going crazy about something. I know it's not this case or budgets; we always lack for resources." Because of his drinking problem and his recovery, he and Kay had come to know Captain Colleen pretty well.

"Bobby, I wish I could tell you, but I really can't." Bobby already had a pretty good idea; there were rumors that IR was investigating a crooked cop.

"It's about Ramsey, isn't it?" Bobby said compassionately. She looked at him, surprised.

"Captain, don't be surprised many of us have known that he's crooked for a while. Take him down our department doesn't need someone like him." Bobby stood up to leave. "Check the bottom of his locker; there's a false bottom you might find something there that will help you." Bobby had seen officer Ramsey lifting a false bottom and putting something in there about a week ago as he turned the corner. He stopped quickly and stepped back to watch, money and a gun were placed inside. Bobby was pretty sure that he hadn't been seen.

The next day Captain Colleen called Bobby and Alex into her office. "I want you guys going up to Minnesota to check out the case they have there."

Both Alex and Bobby were surprised. "I don't think we need to Captain. I think if we get the files, we can get everything we need. And what about the budget?"

"Yes, I'm sure you guys could but I want you to go up there for a couple of days and see if there's anything they missed. You two know this case better than anyone. Why don't you head out tomorrow and don't come back till next Monday use the weekend do some fishing if you want, I hear it's a good state for that. And don't worry about the budget that's my problem." Both were still a little bit surprised, but we're weren't going to turn down the opportunity for some good fishing and the opportunity to personally go over the evidence and talk with the detectives who had handled the case. As they were leaving the office, Colleen called Bobby back. "I want you going to Minnesota because we're going to be taking down Ramsey. We had a bunch of evidence but what you gave us put the final nail in the coffin. We'll be taking him down while you're gone. I don't want anybody in the office thinking it was you who gave us information. With you gone, when this happens, fewer connections will be made, out of sight out of mind. Don't say anything to Alex until he tells you about Ramsey being arrested. That will put a little more distance between you and the evidence even in your partner's mind. One of the IR guys checked out that false bottom last night, and there's about 75 grand and a pistol with the serial number filed off in there. We're going to take him down at one of the shift changes once we get the warrants and everything in place. That's why you're going to Minnesota, but this is between you and me no more words will be spoken, you understand? And stop in and see your old counselor tell him he did a good job with you." Bobby smiled and saw her logic turning in a crooked cop even if he was crooked wouldn't sit well with the rest of the guys. But with him and Alex gone when the takedown occurred would make it harder for them to be connected to it.

Bobby thought to himself, "She's a smart woman, a brilliant woman, in fact! Thank God she's on my side."

The next day they were on a plane to Minnesota. They went directly from getting the rental car to downtown Minneapolis in a meeting with Detectives Peterson and Anderson. Bobby thought to himself, "Peterson and Anderson, the state of "son," Christ, I am back in Minnesota." During his time up at Hazelden, he met a lot of people with "son" attached to their last name. After pleasant greetings, the two officers took them to a room where they had all the evidence laid out. There was little of it. They spent a couple of hours talking about the similarities between all the cases. Peterson and Anderson were sure that whoever had killed Olivia and Harold Danube three years ago had been watching them, but they couldn't find from where.

Bobby spoke up, "We only found his observation post when we moved the search area out to a thousand yards, not the normal 500." Both the "sons" nodded their heads in unison.

46

"Makes sense; we only did the normal 500." They looked at each other. "That makes sense of the small piece of clay we found in the house."

They told Bobby and Alex how they had found a trace of clay in the bedroom that must've come off the killer shoes, but there wasn't any clay in the immediate area. But the detectives told they he probably been watching from the Bluffs above the house. It had a whole different soil content up there.

While copies of the files were being made, the four drove over to Northeast Minneapolis to a little Mexican restaurant "Maya" on Central Avenue. The meal was delicious, and the conversation was pleasant. "We're going to go stay up in Lindstrom. Alex is going to go do some fishing, and I'm hoping to meet and visit my old counselor up at Hazelden." Bobby was always open about his alcoholism and recovery.

"My uncle went through there. It's a good place." Detective Clay Peterson said, looking at Bobby then he turned Alex. "Go to South Lindstrom Lake; that's the best fishing in the area, and you can easily get outfitted there. They're used to out-of-town guests coming in." Soon, Alex had all the information written down of where he could rent a boat and tackle gear. After they said their goodbyes, Alex and Bobby drove up to Lindstrom and checked in at the Comfort Inn and Suites.

Bobby called up to Hazelden and talked with his old counselor, Jim Syverson. Jim invited him to spend the day at Hazelden, sitting in groups with him and attending lectures at Bigelow auditorium. "We'll give you a little tune-up. We'll have lunch and catch up."

The next day Alex was on the lake early, and Bobby met Jim Syverson around 9 o'clock in time for morning group. Bobby loved his old counselor; he was just a very down-to-earth guy, a former hockey player from northern Minnesota. His common-sense talk, and his listening helped the nightmares go away. Jim had taught him how is alcoholism had taken the event and used it to promote the illness inside of him. "Shit, your disease would have you believe that things that aren't your fault are yours!" The words, "Your damn disease runs on shame; it's the gasoline for that." Still echoed in his brain. "You're going to take some guy suicide and make it all about you when it had nothing at all to do with you and everything about him that's alcoholism 101." Jim had taught him well how to hear his illness and to see how it used his mind against him always to create shame and pain that allowed the disease to progress. Jim had told him, "A good alcoholic can make anything about themselves; it's called addictive narcissism. Hell, a good alcoholic can take a thunderstorm and make it personal." It was shortly after these types of talks that the nightmares stopped.

Bobby thoroughly enjoyed today, and Jim was excited to hear that Kay had gone to the meeting when Bobby got his two-year chip. "You two are going to be moving back in together someday you're going to be getting your family back. We call that recovery."

"I'm not so sure of that; she's pretty damn stubborn, and I hurt her pretty good, especially when I put our son in danger."

"Again, alcoholism 101, betray and hurt those you love most for it creates the most shame. You'll be getting Kay back. Why don't you ask her if you can start courting her again. And do it right this time, flowers, chocolates, and take her to nice restaurants she's worth it. I could tell she was a good woman when I met her during family week."

Bobby chuckled to himself; it felt good to be back where is new life had started and spending time with the man who'd helped him reclaim his dignity. With his counselor's help, he came to see he wasn't a bad man, just a man with a bad illness. Bobby, who wasn't a hugger, gave Jim a big hug at the end of the day and left feeling centered and glad for the new choices he was making. He was always amazed at Jim's simple, down-to-earth wisdom and also his ability to make simple sense of things. He got back to the hotel at about the same time Alex was coming back.

Alex had a little cooler of fillets packed in dry ice. "I hit my limit on walleyes and sunfish. Dam good fishing lake! The place where I got the boat and tackle was fabulous! They help me fillet them and get them ready

48

to take back home. Shit, I couldn't put my line in the water and not catch something. It was great!" The two detectives went out for a nice supper, and Bobby filled in and Alex about everything Jim had said to him. "He's right. Kay is going to be letting you back in the house soon. It's a damn good idea to ask her if you can start courting her. She'd like that." That night both slept sound and long.

The next day they had a good breakfast and a leisurely drive back to the airport and then back to Phoenix. As they were sitting in the airport waiting for the plane, Alex, who is checking his phone set out loud. "Jesus Christ, Ramsey has been arrested!"

"What, what you say!" "I got an email from one of the guys, Ramsey's been arrested he was found to be stealing money from drug busts and intimidating drug dealers. He was dirty."

"Shit, which one of us hasn't thought about doing something like that," Bobby said, sounding as sympathetic as he could as they were walking onto the plane.

"Really, but I guess he took it to that next step, the one you're not supposed to. Shit, I did like him, but there was something funny about him. He always did seem more like one of them than one of us." Bobby liked hearing Alex talked this way. He knew that Alex would've done the same if he been in his situation; that's why they made good partners.

As soon as they got back to Phoenix, they went to the house. Most cops called it that because they spent more time there than in their own homes. All the talk was about Ramsey, and it was like that for the next couple of weeks. Bobby was listening, as was Captain Colleen, to see if any connections were being made. None were. The rumors were saying they had gotten an anonymous tip in the mail of somebody saying Ramsey was dirty and to check his locker. Bobby found out later that the whole investigation got started when a merchant took a picture of Ramsey shaking down a drug dealer and pulling out the same gun they had found in his locker and sticking it in the drug dealer's mouth. During the investigation, the drug dealer's DNA was found on the barrel of the gun.

Everybody in the house saw the consequences of Ramsey's action. All of his cases were under review, and some of his perps were having to be released. The mood in the house changed from sympathy to anger for all the extra work falling on everybody's shoulders. Ramsey made a deal when they threatened to put him in the general population at Florence State Prison. Ramsey knew if he was sent to Florence State, he wouldn't last a week, and his death would not have been pretty. Once the deal was struck, and Ramsey was formally in front of the judge, he pled guilty, and he was sent to Wildwood Correctional Complex in Kenai, Alaska under an assumed name. Two months after arriving there, he was found dead, hanging in his cell even though nobody believed it was a suicide, especially with all the bruises on his body. The life expectancy of a crooked cop in a penal system it's about that of a fruit fly. Even though his identity had been changed before arriving at Wildwood, it was clear that his secret had gotten out. Bobby felt no guilt or sense of remorse for a dirty cop is a dirty cop; they deserve a dirty death.

Chapter 9

◆

I could feel a hunger, a growing excitement building inside of me. It had been a good and profitable summer. It was now time to enjoy some of the rewards of my hunts. I so enjoyed cruising in luxury, playing a different role and looking for new victims — my chance to play God who would live who would die. It would also be a time for me to get my head on straight. I had messed up big-time.

I'd gotten stupid, sloppy, arrogant and this needed to change. I was glad these behaviors bothered me so. I committed to myself to not make the same mistake ever again. I even decided there would be no more mints left on pillows at least for two years and after that only sporadically to let the police know that I was still alive, hunting and staying ahead of them. My victims offered little challenge. They were predictably set in their lifestyle. All had a way of making comforts a thing of routine. I always planned well for how to take them down, but still, in my mind, my thoughts were mainly about my real challengers, the detectives whose job it was to find predators like me and take us down.

I was developing a great respect for this Detective Collins and his partner. I'd been researching them as much as I could through my occasional use of the internet. From the details of their cases, I can see they worked well together made the right decisions from good instincts, a dangerous combination. They were a pair of rare cops who enjoyed the hunt as much as I did. And in terms of the murders of Gil and Mary Deutsch and Marvin and Mary Renee Bonan they were making all the right moves. I needed to have the trail go cold. This was another reason I was glad that the Odyssey II would be setting sail in two weeks.

I could relax and enjoy myself once I was on the ship. It was a way I got some of my social needs met. There would be fine dining, beautiful views, fun poker games, excursions, and often I would find and enjoy the company of a woman single or married. I was surprised how many married couples there were with a woman who would gladly take on a cruise lover not caring whether their husband knew or sometimes with the husband's permission. There was even one cruise where I repeatedly made love to a woman in front of her husband as he sat watching sipping on expensive cognac. It was the least I could do after taking him for $35,000 at the poker table I guess he was as lousy a lover as he was a poker player. Each cruise always felt like starting anew. Each was still offering some new adventure. But there was much for me to do.

I drove to the cemetery and found Susan's gravesite. It was raining, so I stayed in the car. The flowers I'd sent rested on the dirt displaced by her coffin mixed in with the other flowers from her funeral. Everything looked nice at her little shrine on the side of the hill. By the mountain of flowers on her grave, it was clear many people had admired her as I had. I paid my respects from afar, taking time to reflect on all the unique kills Susan had unknowingly help me consummate. This would be the last cruise set up for me with Susan's help, so I decided I would make it extraordinary. I would hunt for a special high-end couple deserving of my unique talents and skills. I would make sure that they were rich enough to add significantly to my treasures. This would be my way to honor Susan.

Maybe I would stop after this instead of going through the work of finding and developing a new relationship with a new travel agent. But this was normal for me. Almost always before a cruise I would try and convince myself this would be the last one. Susan's death gave me a new way did try and sell myself on the idea of stopping. But I knew deep inside myself that's all it was a cheap idea, a new trick. That small decent part of myself that moral side of me trying to establish some control. Wanting to offer me a new life. I just laughed at it.

In terms of my home in Idaho, everything had to be locked up and put away; everything had to be secured. I would be gone for a little over two months, a bit longer than usual, but it would be a wonderful cruise. I had always looked forward to traveling to Asia. Believing it would be the right place for me to get lost in, if and when I became too old to hunt.

Years ago I had built a small undetectable room 10 feet under my house tucked away behind three doors and five locks. Inside it was a log of where my treasures were stored and a detailed diary of my adventures that allowed me to remember my kills in great detail. It would be a reward for any detective smart enough to catch me. My diaries would be my legacy; they would stand and let the world know who I was my achievements long after I had died. That's the double bind of a serial killer we build for a legacy, that only can come about by our capture or our death. I wanted people to stand in awe of what I'd done. I believed any true serial killer sought to become a legend. We want our deeds to haunt people and bring fear to them even after we're dead. To have them be afraid that they could someday run into someone like us.

I designed my house so that even from afar, I could set off an "accidental fire" and destroy it if need be. The three doors led to a small room deep ten feet under my house that if there were a fire, it would be safe, most likely undetectable buried under the rubble, a secret just waiting to be discovered. There is a saying, "You're only as sick as your secrets, but in my line of work, you're only as safe as you keep your secrets."

For now, everything needed to be in its place; everything needed to look clean and fresh. I always liked coming home finding my home cleaned and in well-ordered just as I had left it. With all the hidden cameras spread throughout my house and properties, I could stop and check on them at any port of call. But there had never been a problem. I had always found that the best way to prevent a problem was to plan for it.

Looking over the documents of my cruise, I smiled. Susan had made sure that the first night out I would be sitting at the captain's table. It was one of the best ways to be seen without working to be seen. The type of clientele I was looking for always would know who was sitting at the captain's table, and often it was them. I had first met Gil and Mary Deutsch at the captain's table of my last cruise. Mary was impressed that

I knew the designer of her jewelry. And the designer of her dress, Stella McCarthy, Paul McCarthy's daughter. I knew of her, for there had been an article about her in British Vogue. Much of that first evening was spent with Mary and me talking about Ms. McCarthy's skills as a designer, particular the way she used red and green together Mary's two favorite colors. Mary had met Stella at a New York fashion show and over a glass of wine, Stella had told Mary her beliefs on how red was in love with green and green was in love with red. How good lovers always made each other look better.

Mary was a delightful conversationalist. We had such a delightful first night together at the captain's table. She'd repeatedly told me how much she enjoyed our moments together talking about the world. I don't think Mary would say the same for our last moments together.

I found it essential to get close to the wives. They were the gatekeepers. They like hawks, sat perched, keeping watch over their husbands. They more often than not knew how to spot a gold digger or phony, male or female. The men rarely cared anything about style, but they wanted to look successful. So often, they were dressed by their wives like grown-up life-size dolls. The husbands mostly only cared and talked about business and making money. It was the arena they felt most comfortable in; the exception was the men from old money families. They were more accustomed to wealth and the symbols of it than they were in how wealth was created. Many had shame about their inheritance. I went after new money couples.

Coupled with the problem was that old money families and individuals is that they had connections often deep into the fiber of their community so their loss would be much more public and investigated more thoroughly. Lots of the new money individuals or couples had been so busy creating their wealth and establishing themselves that's they hadn't had time to make deep intimate friendships; they often had more acquaintances than friends. At least these were the types I would be hunting. The saying that behind every successful man is a woman often held true with these new wealth couples. Often, making their wealth was a partnership between husband and wife. I felt great affection for these gatekeepers. Some watched over their husbands because that's where the money came from. Most others watched over them out of love and because they knew that their husbands frequently had a naïve quality about them. The skills needed to create wealth aren't exactly the same ones that help you be emotionally and socially mature. Some of these gentlemen were very smart and brilliant but stunted in their emotional intelligence, making them adolescent and immature in their mannerisms. They knew how to push through adversities. Many did not know how to finesse themselves through life, but often that was something their wives had perfected.

Mary had been a "gatekeeper" for Gil out of her genuine affection and love for him. She had great amazement and admiration at what he had created having only in eighth-grade education. Over cigars, whiskey and several hands of poker, Gil told me the story of how his father when Gil was seven-years-old and wanted a bike his father told him to get a job and earn it. Gil had been working ever since. He said that in his garage, he still had that bike hanging there. I stopped in the garage and saw it the night I murdered them. It was a nice bike. It had baskets on the back that Gil had used to deliver groceries from the local grocery store to the elderly or lazy, earning a small delivery fee and often a tip. Gil found he could get a better tip if he brought the groceries in and put them away, especially for some of the elderly clients who used his services. He always had a gift for gab, so he would talk with them and help them not feel lonely, even if it was just for a few brief moments. It was a natural progression for him to move from that bike into owning and developing the vast trucking and moving business they franchised.

One of the last stops I made before departing for San Francisco and the cruise was my old silver mine off of HWY-140 in northern Nevada. Deep within the mine, I kept a 100-gallon sulfuric acid storage tank. Into it, I threw some clothes and paper documents that could've connected me to Susan. I walked deeper into the mine where I had a little office set up. I had a steel chair and wooden desk I had found in an abandoned cabin. I would often go there when I needed quietness to think and develop ideas. I thought about the upcoming cruise and how I wanted to play it; what persona I would take on. Quietness helped me focus. The darkness of the mine helped me go into my darkness, something I found very comforting. Sometimes I would turn off my lantern surrounding myself with quietness and darkness. I needed to leave my life and stepped back into the hunter I was on cruises, a hunter of possibilities and opportunities instead of a hunter of lives, souls and treasures like I had been these last months—time to let the transition come about.

The blackness of the mine always brought me a sense of security, of contentment. I had always lived in darkness ever since I was a child growing up in Florida, always staring into the blackness of my parents' eyes. I guess you could say I was born into darkness, which was my parents' ever-present piercing rage. At best they were always just moments away from a fight, at worst and more commonly they were savagely locked in battle trying to do as much damage to the minds and psychic of each other as they could and then there were the times, they did physical harm to each other. I still remember the flashing lights of the ambulance taking my mother to the hospital the sense of victory in her eyes and the faint smile as she laid on the stretcher the medics wheeling her down the sidewalk as she watched the fear in my father's eyes wondering if he'd be arrested or not. Would she press charges? Even though she threw the first and best punch of the evening, he was at a disadvantage because of his gender and his inability to come across as innocent. He just looked guilty.

The beatings he would regularly give me stop the day I found out that I could use my darkness to scare the man I had always feared. I was eight when I stood in front of my father took one of the kitchen knives made a long gash down my arm blood dripping off my elbow onto the floor, and I told him if he ever touched me again, I would do this to his throat as he slept, I then wished him a good night. I had made it clear to him that even at eight, I was a stone-cold killer waiting for the right moments for it to be released, which would come nine years later. But for now, our roles had been reversed. He was far more afraid of me then I was of him.

I knew that everyone had darkness in their souls most never made friends with it, and few learned how to use it for their advantage. Most pretended they were not of the beast. I remember in one of my readings for I read a lot a prominent psychologist stating that to understand the human being, you must first understand that we humans are animals. I understood, appreciated, and believed this to be true. I decided early on to make friends with my animal side, to form a partnership. I was an animal that preferred the dark shadows. My animal was a good hunter.

My darkness regularly brought me comfort; maybe that's why I always felt quite calm, and at peace, as I watch those I would kill trapped within their fear. It was at those moments I was most at peace for the fear I had felt continuously as a child I had successfully transferred onto and into them. For a few brief moments, we had a special bond. They knew better than anyone the fear I had felt growing up until I decided no more. I had decided to have others feel and experience my pain and fears.

At 11, I was sent to my first foster home. I only stayed there two weeks. I was quickly sent away after I slit the throat of the family dog in front of the couple's birth child after he had tried to bully me. I was sent on to two foster homes at the second one I awoke one night to my foster father sitting on the edge of my bed playing with my genitals I smiled at him, and his head moved down to my lap. When he was done, I told him to be sure and leave $20 on my nightstand. I stayed at that foster home the longest. It was just me my foster parents and one other kid, a redheaded girl named Rita.

It was at 17 that I had my first kill. I'd been working the streets, and some man took me to his house he wanted to be mean to me and make me do things that I didn't want to do that's when he made his mistake. He tried to frighten me. He took out a butcher knife and laid it on the counter and told me if I didn't do as he said he would cut off what hung between my legs. I smiled at him and told him I like he was playing rough that relaxed him enough and changed his focus sufficiently that I could grab the butcher knife and bury it in his heart. Then I, for the first time, felt that addictive calm and peace as I watched him fall to the ground, lay there and his life fade from his eyes. I pulled up a chair sat there staring at him. I was surprised by how comfortable I was in the presence of death. I was thankful for my darkness and how it had saved me once again. I felt no fear, just curiosity. I wasn't worried about getting caught, but I also thought about how I needed to make my presence there unfindable to whoever would be investigating his murder. I then went upstairs and took a shower put on his robe came downstairs and made myself a sandwich. I sat in the living room eating a sandwich and chips the pervert's body so still and quiet laying there not more than 10 feet for me. I fell asleep. I was so relaxed. I woke up during the night got dressed and did away with any presence of myself I had learned on the streets and TV shows that was essential if you didn't want to get caught. After stealing as much as I could put in one of his suitcases I left taking his car driving it to the far side of the city where I wiped it down and left it, I caught a bus I knew would take me back to my apartment. I had gotten enough money and jewelry I lived comfortably for six months.

Chapter 10

◆

Little was being said in the house after hearing about Ramsey's death; everybody was keeping their opinions to themselves. There's always a solid blueline but when it comes to a crooked cop is where you find some gaps in the line. There are those who side with the cop making excuses for them. Then there are the ones like Bobby who make no excuses for a crooked cop believing they get what they deserve. The two camps solved their differences with silence. Someone quickly put a picture of Ramsey up in the duty room. There was black lace draped over it. Nobody disturbed it, but also nobody said anything about it.

In terms of the case, even with the new information for Minnesota, Michigan, and Arkansas, they sat at an impasse. Sandy de Cottle had continued her search and found four more cases that all agreed was probably the work of the same man. The walls in conference room C were filling up, but no one was finding anything strikingly new. There was a frustration setting in. Bobby was finding himself waking up at night thinking about the case. He needed a new way to view the evidence. He and Alex were now being assigned to and working on other cases, solvable cases that needed their time and attention. Every day Bobby would take his lunch break and sit in Conference Room C staring at the pictures wondering what was he missing. He just kept thinking, "I'm going to get you, you, sonofabitch I'm going to get you." The trail was going cold, but at least things were going better with Kay.

After his trip with Alex to Minnesota, Bobby couldn't wait to get home and tell Kay all about it. He called her from the airport and asked if they could go out for coffee, he said to her that he'd had a nice talk with Jim. Kay had always loved Jim after doing the family program at Hazelden.

She couldn't see him that night she was hosting Joe's Boy Scout Troop. They were studying how to tie knots, hoping to earn a new merit badge. And then she had some other things to do. So, it would be a couple of days before she and Bobby could get together. Instead of whining and pushing her to make time for him the new Bobby said, "OK, it'll be nice to see you when you got time. Just let me know I've got some exciting things to tell you or I should say ask you." Not until that weekend were Bobby and Kay able to go out for supper. They spent most of the evening talking about all the details a Bobby and Alex's trip to Minnesota. At one point, Bobby swallowed hard and said, "Jim said I ought to ask you if it's okay to court you again. He said the relationship we had is gone and we need to start a new as if we're dating."

He looked at her. "So, what do you think?"

Kay played hard to get like she had when they first met said, "What do I think about what?"

Bobby knew that she would make him ask her directly. There was no getting around it. Especially after what he had put her through.

"Miss Kay Collins, I would like your permission to start courting you, would you be willing to go out on a date with me?"

She smiled. "Let me think about it. Give me a call in a couple of days. I'll give you my answer then." By the look on her face, they both knew what the answer would be, but she was going to leave him dangling twisting in the air. That night when she drove home, she stopped it the drug store and bought a thank you card wrote a little note in it. "Jim, Thanks for everything he's doing well, I'm doing well in Al-Anon and most of all Joe's glad to have his father back. I will always love you for what you've done for us, our family. Love Kay -- P.S.: The courting was a great idea! He asked me tonight for permission to court me; I'm making him sweat a bit." Kay addressed the envelope put a stamp on it and sent it off to Minnesota.

Ever since getting back from Minnesota, Bobby had a different air about him. He was not his grouchy old self actually he smiled quite a bit and even made some jokes, bad ones, but they were still jokes. One day Captain Colleen had had enough of his cheeriness she looked at him. "What the hell is going on? Your little Mr. Sunshine's attitude is driving me crazy!"

Bobby just smiled. "Kay is going to let me court her."

Captain Collins laughed. "Oh, so that's was going on, you're getting laid. Good for you, good for the two of you, but mostly good for JC."

"No! No! We're not doing any of that." For some strange reason, he didn't want the captain getting some's notion that Kay was easy and that they were having sex. "I'm just bringing her chocolates, flowers, sending her a card once a week, and taking her out for a nice dinner. That's what my old counselor told me to do."

"Smart man, good advice."

She kept laughing as she walked out of the room then she turned around casually, asking, "Mr. Sunshine, you didn't happen to talk to him about the case and see if he had any thoughts." Bobby hadn't even thought of anything like that; they were in two separate worlds. He shook his head no. The captain had recently been to one seminar that pushes people to look at things from a different perspective when struck, an "out of the box seminar." They were made to do an exercise where they took one of their problems then had to think about it as if they were a baker. She felt the activity at first was stupid and was surprised when it gave her a new insight into the personal issue she was struggling with. "Why don't you, we're stuck and maybe a new set of eyes, a different brain might help, at least it couldn't hurt, and hell you're always easier to be around after you've talked to him. Annoying, but easier."

That afternoon Detective Collins called up to Hazelden. His old counselor was in a group, but the unit secretary said she would make sure he got the message. It wasn't more than 30 minutes later, and Jim

61

Syverson was on the phone. "Hey buddy what's the news, is she going to let you court her?"

"Yes, every week I'm sending her cards, getting her flowers she likes that, but she had me stop with the chocolates she was starting to put on weight, great advice as always, it's working out nicely."

"Well, that is AA the Third Step turning your will and life over to CARE. It's a dam good step." Bobby knew if he didn't interrupt Jim, he was going to be getting a 15-minute lecture on the healing powers of a life turned over to Care, as Jim had pronounced many times before. "Let Care be your GPS."

"Jim I'm doing as you taught me care, care, care, Let go Let God, Easy Does It, and it works if you work it, but that's not why I'm calling you. I've got something else I wanted to talk to you about." There was a curious silence on the other end.

"I'm calling you about a case I'm working on, a serial killer. We're completely stuck. I need a new set of eyes. My Captain, she's a good hard-core Al-Anon lady she's the one who got Kay into Al-Anon, for some reason after me telling her about you and your advice she thinks you're kind of a smart guy, go figure. She suggested that you may have a different way of seeing or framing what we're seeing. Ever since she went to a conference about six months ago, she's big on having fresh eyes. I know you can't talk about cases, but we're not under any of those restrictions, we don't have any damn HIPAA (Health Insurance Portability and Accountability Act of 1996) laws holding us back. Might you be willing to look at everything we have on this serial killer and give us your thoughts? We do need fresh eyes. I figure that with what you do your kind of a profiler, I know you sized me up pretty quickly. We could pay you for your time."

Again, there was quietness on the other end, Jim finally spoke up, "Damn, that sounds interesting, really interesting! I'm never done anything like that before. Profiler Jim Syverson sounds good and kind of fun! Sure, I will I'll be glad to help in any way I can, but I don't know how much help I'll be. But don't insult me with this; you'll pay me stuff. You're staying sober and stopping by to see me is payment enough. I've got a couple of meetings coming up so I can't talk too long now, but why don't we set up a time for later probably three or four hours and talk about it. Do I get a badge? I've always wanted a badge?"

Bobby chuckled, "Jim, do you mind if I send down some crime pictures, with the case notes, to give a look-see? I'd like you to get a clear picture of what the killer left behind and how he staged it; he's got a flair for the dramatics. I'd like you to look at them and see how you make sense of them, I've got my way of looking at them, but I'd like your input you've always had a different way of seeing things. But I've got a warn you they are kind of gruesome, you know people don't look so good after they taken two bullets to the head."

"Bobby, I was in Desert Storm, so there isn't much I haven't seen. Absolutely send it all up to me. I'll take a look at everything, sit with it all for a couple of days, and then give you any feedback and thoughts I have." That afternoon Detective Collins put together a package of all the case notes and photos of the crime scenes for fun he stopped at the toy store in got a plastic detective badge and threw it in a US Priority Mailbox and dropped it at the post office on his way back to his apartment.

Bobby went back to his apartment, cleaned up and headed out for Wednesday date night with Kay. Now every Wednesday Joe would have a sleepover at his friend Anthony's house so Bobby and Kay could go out—courting. He stopped at the flower shop first getting her a bouquet of lilies which he had recently found out were her favorite flowers. On one of their recent outings he was enjoying, a store had a bouquet of lilies out, and Kay stopped to smell them telling the salesclerk they were her favorite flowers and that she always wore Stargazer Lilly perfume. Bobby, just thought to himself, "So that's what that smell is. I've always liked it." He was realizing how oblivious he'd been to Kay and probably most of the world.

Jim's words went through his head, "Alcoholism 101!"

Bobby got to the house rang the doorbell, and Kay answered it. She was wearing a sundress blue with yellow flowers; the colors made her blond hair sparkle. The cut of the dress showed off her cleavage well. She hadn't dressed this provocative with Bobby in years. "How'd you know I like lilies?"

"Your perfume honey you always smell like lilies." Bobby was so proud of himself he could see he was racking up husband points left and right and helping Kay kill off some of the resentments she must have had from the years of him being consumed with only himself, his pain, and Scotch. "Plus, I heard you tell that saleslady over at "Old Things and New Things" last week it was your favorite flower."

Kay raised her eyebrows to show Bobby she was impressed, grabbed the flowers held them to her breast a leaned over and kissed him on the cheek. Bobby could feel a tear about an inch behind his eyes even if it was only a peck on the cheek. She hadn't kissed him in years. "Where are we going tonight?" Kay asked part of the new rules Bobby had to pick out where they would eat.

"There's a new Mexican restaurant, and I know how much you like Mexican so I thought we'd try it out." Bobby looked a Kay for her reaction.

"We don't have to. I know you don't like Mexican."

"Honey truth be known during these past couples of years whenever I was missing you, I would go to your favorite Mexican restaurant and have a meal I've found that I like it. It goes particularly well with crow and humble pie something I've had to eat a lot of these past years." They walk to the car Kay waited for Bobby to open the door.

When they got to the restaurant, it was hot out, so Bobby offered to drop Kay at the door, and she said, "No, I'd rather walk with you." Once they parked the car, she held out her arm as she had during their younger years, Bobby hooked his arm with hers, and they walked into the restaurant. As she was walking to the door, Kay looked her clean-shaven husband in the eyes. "Sweetie, I really want you to know how much I appreciate how you're working to change, I really do, and you're not half bad at this dating thing." But the only word Bobby heard was, "Sweetie" she hadn't used it with him in years. This time the tears weren't an inch behind his eyes but in the corners.

As soon as they got in the door looking away, he said, "Excuse me, Kay, I've got to go to the bathroom." As soon as he got in the door, the tears rushed out, and he pounded on the wall. "Jesus Christ, get it together you don't want to blow it now." He told himself. But his wife's sweet touch and words have brought to the surface all of the missing of the last few years.

"Goddamn feelings! Goddamn feelings!" Then the thought rushed through his head, "If there's ever a time for a drink, it's now." It helped get his attention, and it scared him, but he laughed almost as quickly he could hear Jim Syverson's voice, "Alcoholism 101 have a feeling, take a drink."

He just splashed some water on his face took a paper towel and wiped his face clean, still smiling and chuckling to himself. As he got to the table, Bobby looked at Kay she had a look of concern he smiled. "It's all these damn diet cokes they go right through me." He could tell she wasn't buying it. "Honey, it just feels so nice your touch, your kind words it all got to me I needed to go into the restroom and have a good cry."

Her hand reached out and touched his. "It's okay. You can cry with me if you want. I've seen you cry before. Damn the last time I saw you cry was when Joe was born." They looked at each other this time a tear ran down Kay's cheek. "I think we're going to make it honey, I think we're going to make it." They sat silently, staring at each other, enjoying the moment until it was interrupted by a waitress.

"Welcome to "South of the Border," do you care for some drinks? We've got a special on margaritas?" Bobby looked at her. "I'll have a Diet Coke no ice with some lime I don't drink." Kay just looked at her. "I'll have the same but ice in mine."

Once she had left, Bobby said to Kay, "It was so funny in the bathroom when the tears were coming, the first voice to go through my head was, 'If I ever needed a drink it was now' the second voice going through my head was Jim's saying..." and as he was saying it, Kay chimed in, "Alcoholism 101 have a feeling take a drink." They laughed. The tension that had started to surround the table was gone.

"I wanted to let you know I sent a package of information about this case, the serial killer, up to Jim to look at. Captain Colleen suggested it, thought a pair of totally fresh eyes might help us see something we're missing."

He could tell from the look in Kay's eyes she found the idea intriguing. "What did he think about it?"

"He seemed excited to do it. You know he is kind of an investigator in his own way."

"Yeah, I guess you're right. He sure figured out what was killing you." They kept holding hands until their food arrived. The date was a success.

Chapter 11

◆

As I walked up the gangplank of the Odyssey II, I felt my persona changing; it brought a smile to my face. The captain, Captain Del Monty, was there to greet me, I expected nothing less, for I had had Susan book me into the owner's suite. He introduced me to Angela, a woman in her early 30s who would be my attendant 24 hours a day, and my personal concierge for the entire voyage. She smiled pleasantly and bowed slightly in my direction. She was of Asian descent. For a second, I was thrown off balance. This woman had a strange effect on me; I immediately felt calm and joyful in her presence. Something rare for me. After pleasantries, the three of us walked to my cabin, and Captain Del Monty told me about Angela's Vietnamese heritage and how comprehensive her knowledge about the Asian continent and the many cultures in bedded within it. "Angela is very knowledgeable, but she takes a special interest in Vietnam if there's anything you'd like to know about it she's the one to ask. Be sure and have her be your guide when we stop there."

I looked at her, and she had a pleasant humble smile as the captain went on informally bragging about her talents and knowledge. There was a hint of Jasmine coming from her not overpowering or underpowering just enough to be enjoyable. She worked on casting the smallest shadow possible, but clearly, she was studying everything about me as I was with her. As we walked into the owner suite, I noticed under the bar area; there was a safe with the door open I walked over and put my briefcase in it, set the combination and closed it. Not a word was said by the captain or by Angela.

The captain showed me around the suite talking constantly; he was a talker; he took me out on the balcony of pointed out the Golden Gate

Bridge and Alcatraz. "Will be passing under her around 6:30 tonight as we make our way out of the harbor make sure you're outside; it's quite a view something that I still enjoy to this day."

The captain and I sat down almost instantly Angela brought us each a Corona Extra and a bowl of seasoned cashew nuts. "This is your favorite beer if I'm correct?" Angela asked.

"You've done your homework well, yes, it is, and as you seem to know, I love cashews, especially fresh ones with a little bit of sea salt just like these." The captain smiled at her competency.

We sat talking pleasantries me asking him about the voyage and him relishing getting to give me his little presentation on the Odyssey II. "She's the best ship I've ever sailed, she's the best in her class by far." Captain Del Monty went on about all the details that made the Odyssey II the most magnificent ship he had ever commanded. I politely listened and nodded my head at the appropriate times and ask questions that would keep him talking. But my attention was on Angela. She was watching my every move working to come to know who I was and what my needs seem to be. The captain with his large hands grabbed a massive handful of cashews as did I and almost immediately, Angela disappeared with the bowl and as quickly returned it full to the brim. She stood there motionless but taking everything in. After about 15 minutes, Captain Del Monty excused himself saying he had to get back to his duties of preparing the ship for departure, leaving Angela and myself out on the balcony.

I motion for her to sit down and she politely declined, but I insisted, "Angela if you're going to be my attendant for two months then you need to know certain things about me. One of them is that I treat staff with respect and dignity."

"I already know that, sir."

"Angela no more calling me sir it makes me feel so old and I'm not quite there yet." She smiled! My name is Daniel, Daniel Ray; many people call me Dan."

"I would prefer to call you Daniel I don't like when good names get shortened up." She had read me well.

"Again, please sit down so we can talk." I gestured for her to sit down. "Thank you, Daniel."

She did, I excuse myself telling her I would be back in a second. I returned with a Corona Extra and handed it to her. "I'm making the assumption that you drink."

She smiled at me. "Very, very little, but I do like a good beer or Margarita now and then."

"Would you prefer a beer or a margarita during our afternoon visits."

"Margarita."

"Then please have the bar stocked with top-shelf tequila."

"I do need to go over some items." I smiled, nodded and she for the next ten minutes told me details of everything that she could do for me, how I just needed to dial the number "789," and she would answer it anytime. She took the iPad that was under her arm and gave it to me. "Compliments of the company it's yours to keep after the voyage. I can set it up for you just tell me what user name you would like to use."

I handed it back to her. "It's yours now, I rarely do computers or other electronic things. I don't want my name associated with it put yours in you can keep it. Plus, I will want you to research some things for me at times, can you do that? It may be about other guests."

"Absolutely Daniel, and what we talk about in private nobody else will know I guarantee you. Discretion absolute and total discretion during this voyage and after. If anyone asks me you've never taken a voyage on our company to my knowledge. Other attendants gossip I don't." All this was very nice to hear, and something about her reassured me that she was telling the truth, but of course, I was going to test her.

"I on these cruises I play poker for high-stakes. It's just something I relish. So, having information even a little bit of information about other players their mannerisms, their little secrets, can be helpful to me. So, I will look forward to us having these daily afternoon meetings." Where we get together, I'll have a beer and you a Margarita. And I do make a mean Margarita. I'll be very interested about the things I want you to tell me. I want you to tell me about the guests and all the latest gossip."
She giggled. "It gets pretty juicy and naughty sometimes."

"That's the type I like best." She giggled again.

Angela looking directly into my eyes, "But you must remember ships are like little towns where everybody knows everybody's business. I hope you don't become a juicy little tidbit for someone to enjoy during their afternoon tea or morning coffee." I got the sense that Angela had heard about some of my past escapades.

"I'll try. I'll try not to embarrass you---too much." It was pleasant banter, but each word was an exchange of information as we checked each other out.

"Can we make our afternoon meetings at a regular time that will help me in my duties."

"How about 3 o'clock that'll give us time to discuss anything if needed and for me to have time to clean up for supper and maybe even take a nap."

"Very good."

She then went on telling me how the bar would be stocked with my preferred brands. "You enjoy a glass of Macallan Rare Cask Single Malt Scotch Whisky after supper."

I laughed. "Again, you done your homework well! How many ice cubes do I like in my glass?" I joked.

She joked back. "Three if I remember correctly."

I clapped my hands. "Well done! Well done!"

"I'm drinking less nowadays, so you don't have to have it that well-stocked."

She went on telling me how there would be a reserved seat for me in the main dining room for all three meals and to let her know if I needed a bigger table to entertain guests or when I prefer to be alone.

"Breakfast I always prefer to be alone. I like Eggs Benedict and to read the morning paper."

"You like three eggs instead of two on your English muffins lightly toasted, and you like the New York Times, is that correct?"

She already knew the answer, but it was polite of her to ask. "Yes."

"Tonight, you'll be at the captain's table and any other night should you like to dine there you'll always be welcome, just let me know."
I sighed. My God is he a talker, one of those nervous talkers. She giggled but didn't agree with me letting me know she would not betray or say anything against her boss. "I'll be at the table tonight, but after that, I'll only show up if there's going to be someone interesting, and I'll leave that up to you. If you tell me I should dine at the captain's table, I will, and I assume I'll be seated next to the person who you think might interest me." Angela nodded her head, totally understanding. Something about her comforted me.

Then she asked me, "Daniel, everything I know about you comes from our records from past cruises, but I also did a Google search of you, I thought you should know."

"You made it clear to me that you done your homework and done it extremely well but thank you for telling me. Was your question?"

"There's very little it just says that you're a very wealthy man in northern Canada who is a bit of a recluse."

"All accurate. I made my money early in life, private investments in the stock market, and I don't like much attention. Recluse, that's an interesting word, but I guess it's accurate." I chuckled. I had paid good money for my passport and identity. The man who monitored it would now and then post something about me that gave little or no information. "I like to travel and see different parts of the world, and I like to play high-stakes poker cruising allows me to do both."

"And you're quite a good poker player from what I hear. You know our high-end clients get known amongst us. Many attendants talk you know that, but again I reassure you I'm one of the few that knows how to be discreet. I listen much more than I talk."

I then reached in my wallet and took out ten $100 bills and handed it to Angela. "You also must know I tip well and I do like to hear all the gossip, especially about those that I'll up against in poker. All poker players like an edge. If you need any money to give other attendants for information, let me know." Angela bowed slightly took the hundreds folded them in half, and with her small petite hand reached down inside the top of her uniform and placed them inside her bra. There would've been room for more bills for she was very delicate and small breasted.

"I'll be glad to get and give you is much information as I can. So far, I know Pete Jamerson and Henry Sanford will be on the cruise. I know you played against them in the past." The names brought back memories. Henry Sanford fancied himself a poker player when he, in reality, was just a bit above average he would be good for a few thousand dollars. Pete Jamerson was an outstanding poker player. He would make the games exciting. "Pete is a good player, can you find out if he booked his trip before me or after me. I wonder if he came to play against me." She nodded. "I'll have that information for you tomorrow." "I'm assuming his wife is with him. She's a pleasant woman, Magdalene." "Yes, she is signed up for the cruise, neither of them happens to be on board yet."

I smiled at her. She, like Susan, was very competent with her job. I hoped she didn't have to meet the same fate as Susan. "I know you attendants are a close-knit group please get as much information as you can while giving as little information about me as possible. Truthfully, I'm not that vain but, I do want to hear what others are saying about me. Again, all this little information may be helpful for me in my poker games. It may help me learn the tell of my opponent. Or I may throw out a little piece of juicy gossip right at a time where I want my opponent to lose concentration. All this helps in small ways as I look for any advantage over the other players. All poker players do this and if they say differently than they are either a liar or they're not really a poker player. Angela, you'll find out if there is one thing I take seriously, it's my poker."

She was smiling truly enjoying the conversation then she looked at her watch. "Excuse me, Daniel, there're some things I must do. I'll check in later. Remember there will be the lifeboat drill shortly before the ship leaves port. It's mandatory for everyone, even for those staying in the owner's suite," she said it as if she was apologizing, but I knew she was doing her duty. "You mean with the owner suite I don't get my own personal lifeboat in case there's trouble, it's an outrage!" Angela laughed; she enjoyed that I was making fun of the obnoxiousness that the wealthy often displayed. She bowed lightly as she excused herself.

I sat watching the busyness of the harbor. Two tugboats were steering a larger vessel away from its mooring positioning the vessel so it could start its journey. There was a smell of diesel in the air and the sound of seagulls and engines mixed. I sat curious wondering what this journey would bring.

73

Chapter 12

◆

About a week and a half after Bobby had sent the package up to his old counselor, they set up a call. He and Alex and Captain Colleen we're sitting in conference room C, and at the last minute, they also invited Sandy de Cottle to attend they were all enjoying her cocky little attitude. Bobby started the meeting off. "Hey Jim, thanks for doing this. Just to let you know who's in the room, there's Alex. You met him up at Hazelden."

Jim answered, "Hey, Alex." Alex greeted him back.

"There's my Captain Colleen Donahue."

"Hi, Colleen are you the black belt Al-Anon lady I heard about?"

Everybody smiled except Sandy who had no idea what they're talking about. "Yes, I am, my dad was a drunk he got sober through a program down here. He attended the "Meadows of Tucson" it took the first time. He's been sober nineteen years still going to meetings and got a platoon of pigeons. I started in Al-Teen back then."

"Meadows out of Tucson I've heard of it they say it's a good program."

Colleen chimed in, "At least it was for him never worked for my mom. She's a drunk too. She didn't make it; she still out there, a Skid Rower."

"So, you got hit with both sides of the bat." Jim shot back.

Colleen chuckled, "I guess that's one way to say it."

Everybody was smiling and relaxing except for Sandy who sat there looking dumbfounded learning more about her coworkers and boss then she ever had known and not knowing what to do with it.

Bobby broke in. "Jim, there's also a new young officer who is a whiz with computers Sandy de Cottle is with us she is the lady who combed the internet and found the other cases spread out across the states and from the look on her face she has no idea what we're talking about."

They all laughed, and Sandy shook her head in agreement.

"Hi, Sandy, nice to meet you, maybe when we've finished here, I can talk to you about why my computer keeps shutting down."

Sandy being the problem solver she was quickly shot back. "It's probably one to the settings you probably have it set to turn off way too quickly so if you pause too long it thinks you're not using it."

Jim laughed. "I like her already, a true fixer. Yes, teach her about all this recovery stuff; she probably got somebody who drinks too much in her life."

Sandy blurted out, "My mom, I can't seem to get her to stop. But she's promised me she will."

Jim said, "Colleen, did you hear that I think that is your department." Everyone was laughing except for Sandy.

"Yes, Jim I heard, I'll get on her case right away. But were all wanting to hear what you think about our crazy."

"Oh, I don't think he's crazy, super crazy dangerous but not crazy, crazy. Probably tests in the high IQ range maybe even off the charts."

"What do you see?" Bobby chimed in.

"I'm sitting here with all the case notes and all the pictures you sent me. Do you mind if I ramble and if you got questions ask me?"

Captain Colleen threw in, "Any way you want to do this is fine with us."

Jim started talking. "As you know, I see it through an addiction counselor's mind. He's an addict a hard-core addict."

Alex threw the question out there, "If he's addicted to what? We've never found any hint of drugs or anything like that?"

"Alex, he's not addicted to anything like drugs or alcohol that would get in the way of his true addiction. He's addicted to the most powerful drug there is hate. It consumes him, he's angry all the time, but his type of anger sharpens his mind not dulls it like with most people. Most of us, when we get angry, immediately get thrown into our egos. We get dumber often say stupid things. I know I do. We go to our primitive brain. This guy gets angry, and it sends him up to his smart brain, thinking brain, a rare and dangerous combination. It excites him makes him feel good. He lives to outthink, outsmart people, hate is his drug. His's true rush comes when he watches them die. He's wired differently than we are.
He's angry 24 hours a day like a heroin addict always high, and he loves it. He's a brilliant man; you have to respect him but so, so dangerous."

Bobby piped in, "Any idea what he is so angry about."

"Bobby, I think that's where you guys and I think about it differently. You ask was he so angry about it. I ask who taught him to be so angry. Anger and killing are not a problem for him; it's a solution. I would bet a dime to a dollar that his first kill was some time when he was in adolescence. He's probably been on his own for a long time. Any of you ever seen the movie Tombstone?"

Everybody's head was shaking, yes. "Yeah, we all have, Jim, why?"
"There's a scene in that movie; Doc Holliday is laying in the bed of that

76

rancher played by Charlton Heston. Then Wyatt Earp asks Doc Holiday about Johnny Ringo. 'What makes a man like him tick? And Earp asks Doc Holliday, 'What is he so angry about?' And Doc Holiday answers back, 'Being born! Wyatt being born. You've got yourself a Johnny Ringo here. A man who gets smarter and quicker and more dangerous the angrier he gets.'" Sandy was furiously taking notes.

"So, you think he was abused?" Colleen asks.

"I'm sure he was and severely may have even killed his father or mother, but I would bet his father. I believe he watched his mother get physically abused. That's why I think he kills the wife first wants the husband to see, or more accurately he wants his father to see that he's better at being angry then he is or to see his mother being relieved of life with such a horrible man is over. His way of protecting her he sees her as weak and vulnerable, and she might quite well have been."

"Do you think he experienced sexual abuse?" Sandy asked.

"No, I don't think so, at least not at home if he ever got placed in the foster care system, maybe there's a lot of sexual abuse that takes place in some of those homes. But I believe this is about reenacting what he grew up with and he's not leaving any messages about growing up with sexual abuse. Even after he'd ripped the women's nightgowns or blouses open, he covered them back up when he put them in their beds. That's why I think both he and his mother were abused, by his father. He treats the women kinder with more respect. Some of the men who it looks pushed back up against him or resisted his requests were beaten up worst. But with the wives killing them first is an act of kindness for them, setting them free of their husbands. When he did burn that one woman's breasts, there was nothing sexual about it, it was just a way to get the husbands to talk, probably give up the location or combination of a safe. Probably one of those statements. 'If I can do this to your wife, just think what I'll do to you.'"

So, you think he's been killing for a long time.

77

I'm almost sure of it; I also believe he's been on his own for a long time. He has probably lived on the streets for a while.

"What about our age assessment?" Alex piped in.

"I agree with your age assessment. Sandy should start researching abuse cases that made it to child protection when he would have been four, five, six, or seven. With this much hatred, I have no doubt it was probably pretty severe, so there may have been some child abuse reports. It's a place to start."

"It seems like he kills about once or twice a year, but we've got some longer gaps."

"Sandy, keep researching, he's probably got more kills somewhere we haven't found yet. I'm sure he's killing one or two times a year-- at least."

"What about the damn mints?" Colleen leaned over and loudly said into the speakerphone in the middle of the table.

"You guys know that he's just taunting you, playing with you. He most likely sees you as his father. He wants to show you how smart he is and how stupid you are compared to him, excuse my language, but he probably sees you as just dumb cops. If he starts to see you as smart, that will only anger him more and also excite him more. He's not the first killer with daddy issues that get played out on the police.

"Or mommy issues!" Colleen piped in. We're getting more and more that all the time.

"The mint it's a clue maybe he worked in some high-end hotels you know the type that leaving mints on your pillow. Maybe that's where he hunts. Maybe his folks worked at a hotel. I don't know, but I know it is important. It's his signature; it is him bragging to you and challenging you."

"And where do we find him? It's a big nation, you know?" Alex asked.

"I have no idea where you find him now, but if you can find out where his first couple of kills was that's where I would start. His first kill was probably an individual unless it was his parents check there first, guys who killed their parents, but my guess it wasn't."

"I was just telling everybody earlier I found two more kills that seemed similar to his right on the edge of what he does from years ago, with the couple there was no mint on the pillow; otherwise, everything else was identical. Because of how clean the crime scene was the local police connected him to another person, but they're not sure if they're connected. A single guy killed with a knife, but no evidence even though he made a sandwich and took a shower. The detectives said they had never seen a murder scene with not a spot of evidence before, totally clean even after making a sandwich and taking a shower. Crazy isn't it" Sandy threw out.

"Interesting they're not in the information I have?"
"No.
I just discovered it them last week."

"Where were they?"

"Both down in Florida, one on Marco Island, one in a town area called New Smyrna Beach. The couple on Marco Island were wealthy and the guy in New Smyrna Beach he was upper-middle-class."

"So, let's just play it out like it's our guy. It's probably not but let's just play it out. The New Smyrna Beach would have been the first kill of the two." Jim asked.

"Yes, why do you say that?"

"It was probably his first, and he found something in there that sparked the idea of what he would hunt for. It was probably because of

79

the items he found in that house that he decided to become a murderer/burglar. Any valuables taken?"

"Yes, monies, Rolex and jewelry. Sandy responded.

"And a bigger haul with the couple?" Jim asked

"You're dead on, gold coins the couple had just under 70 ounces in gold coins so said their son. All gone. The police thought maybe the son just took them or said they had these coins when they didn't, so he could report them to the insurance company and get paid or get paid twice."

"No, I bet your guy took them not the son. Then the guy started seeing how he could provide for himself by robbing and killing."
"I'd start looking around New Smyrna Beach, then check out the central region of Florida. That might be where he grew up. Sandy is it?"

"Yes?"

"I would check out all the severe child abuse cases in Central Florida and then the rest of Florida you may get a lead down there. But remember it's most likely not our guy, but at least will learn a lot."

"Thanks, it gives me a place to start," Sandy said with some relief.

"He's making a dam good living, but always remember it's the murders that he is all about. But like I said he's incredibly smart knows it takes a lot of money to help keep himself comfortable and safe."

"Jim, we don't think he's got any military background do you agree or disagree?" Bobby asked.

"I agree. But it's too bad that he didn't find a way into the military with his skills and having little remorse he would've been perfect for a Delta team. It's too bad they didn't find him quick enough. They're always looking for recruits like him.

There was silence; everybody was sitting thinking, taking in, processing the conversation. After a bit, Jim piped up.

"Is this being tape-recorded?"

"No, Sandy's taking notes like a maniac but know this isn't being recorded," Bobby answered.

"Put your pen down. Sandy, what I'm going to say I want no record of. I'm going to say it, but I've never said it!" Jim hesitated for about thirty seconds. "If and when you catch him, and I pray to God you do, you need to put him down. No second thoughts, no hesitation. He'll come at you fast and strong if cornered. You have to put him down. He's already thought of how he would do it. If you find his house watch out if he knows anything about explosives it'll be booby-trapped. Killing a police officer is probably something he dreams of, again daddy issues. He plans out everything, even the way he wants to die. No tasers, live rounds and fast, fire fast and accurate he will be. Understand?"

Sandy spoke up, "We're bound by due process. Maybe we can use tasers, or he'll surrender when we corner him." The rest of the team looked at each other.

"I'm a great believer in due process, but with him, due process will get you killed. He probably tasers himself regularly so that he is used to the effects and can quickly shake them off. Please know HE WILL NOT SURRENDER. If he's acting as if he will, that's just what he is doing acting, creating a moment or two to figure out who he'll kill first, second and third. He is more beast and demon than human." Captain Donahue, Bobby, and Alex were respectfully quiet; the three of them knew that Jim was right saying what needed to be said. They all had been in this business long enough to have lost colleagues and friends to the type of innocence that Sandy still carried.

Sandy sighed. "If we put him down without due process, aren't we just like him?"

81

Jim understood her innocence, but he also knew that it gave an advantage to whoever they were hunting.

"Sandy, none of us are like or could ever be like him only in form. Sandy, you could have lunch with him. He would shoot you in the face, continue with his meal, order and eat dessert, then go home and take a nap. Bullets kill, and so does innocence."

Trying another argument, Sandy added, "But he puts them in bed and left them looking so nice and peaceful, yes he murders them but not in some perverse way."

"Sandy, it's all about his mental issues. It's his way of being kind to his mother. But if in his sick fantasy, if his sick mind needed them to be skinned alive and then left hanging by their thumbs, that's what he would have done. There is not a decent cell in his body."

Sandy, not knowing how to respond, just said, "So you've dealt with guys like him before?"

Jim's mind floated back to Desert Storm, then he spoke up. "Ronald Nokk, he was an E4 in my unit in Desert Storm. He was a smart, handsome young lad, brilliant like the man we're dealing with. But after his first kill, something snapped inside of him. He fell in love with taking lives. All he ever thought about was how to murder, main, torture the enemy, how to frighten them, intimidate them, and act out his insanity on them. We were all scared to death of him but also glad he was part of our unit. I saw him go out one night when we were being surrounded by an elite Iraqi unit. The next morning, he walked back into camp entirely covered in blood with a match hanging out of the corner of his mouth. He immediately went to the mess tent and sat there covered in blood, having a huge breakfast for he was famished and then he cleaned up. When we went out on patrol that morning, we found out that the unit had moved on. We also found 14 Iraqis, naked, piled together, all of their teeth were missing, you could hear them rattling around in a bag that Ronald attached to his side. All of them had been castrated. He did all this to frighten the enemy to have them move out of our area, and it worked. He personally killed more men than the rest of our unit combined. When the war was over, and it was time for us all to go home, Ronald slid out into the desert. We never saw him again. He didn't come home with us. He's probably still out there. He was reported missing in action."

Jim didn't tell Sandy or the rest of them the entire truth. The rest of our unit and probably Ronald himself knew we couldn't be sending someone like him back to the states. In those last weeks, knowing we were all to go back home one day on patrol, Jim put a bullet in the back of Ronald's head. Jim held his friend in his lap for they were good friends. As Ronald laid there dying, he stared up at Jim with a smile on his face; his last words were, "I'm glad it was you!" Not a word was said by the rest of the unit. All standing respectfully and reverently around Ronald, this killing machine had saved their lives many times over, but they all knew that what was done needed to be done, even Ronald.

Putting his friend down like a mad dog, for Jim and Ronald, we're great friends during the war, was part of what sent Jim deep into his demons and his alcoholism. He never talked about it until he got to treatment. The first time he ever talked about it with another person was during his fourth and fifth steps with the priest towards the end of treatment. The priest suggested that every day, Jim light a small candle and pray for Ronald. Jim made a little shrine in his house with the picture of Ronald and him together in Iraq. There was a candle he would light and say his morning prayers, always giving thanks and asking for forgiveness. Soon after he did this "remembrance and honoring ritual" as the priest called it, the nightmares stopped, he got sober, and eventually became a counselor.

To this day, he still lights the candle and says a prayer for Ronald, but he doesn't ask for forgiveness anymore. One day a man had appeared at Jim's house, it was Ronald's brother, he didn't stay. He said that his brother had visited him in a dream told him to find Jim, given him his name, he was to tell me, "Thank you! You did what needed to be done." The man delivering the message didn't ask for an explanation. He just turned and walked away as if he knew everything.

83

Sandy threw out, "Well, that was war."

Both Captain Donahue and Bobby simultaneously said, "And so is this, and so is this."

Pleasantries were said with Captain Donahue thanking Jim for his insights, making it clear that he had been a great help.

"We'll start searching around New Smyrna Beach. If and when we catch this killing machine. I'll send you a real badge, Detective Collins told me about the plastic one he slipped in the package he sent you. Thanks again, I bet you're a dam good counselor, you would've made a wonderful detective. My grandfather told me, he was a Vietnam vet, they too had someone like Ronald in his unit in Nam. He just slipped away one night into the jungle. My grandfather and me often wondered how many men like Ronald that wars have created."

"Many, I'm sure there were many." Jim quietly whispered into the phone.

"I'll work on Sandy with her codependency and naïveté. I'll get her out of her research room and her computer. I'll have her see some of the things we deal with daily. You're right if she keeps that innocent and naïveté, she could be dangerous to herself and others if and when she's called out into the field, she's too good we can't afford to lose her because of her innocence," Captain Donahue said, staring directly at Sandy when she said this. Sandy sat there quietly fidgeting in her chair.

After the phone was hung up, the four sat there and started strategizing what to do. Sandy would research family murders, and severe child abuse down in Central Florida from Dayton Beach down to Cape Canaveral from 1970 to 1985. New Smyrna Beach sat directly between these two areas approximately 50 to 60 miles from each.

Chapter 13

◆

The announcement was made for all passengers to grab their life vests and go to their staging areas. Daniel Ray grabbed his vest and exited his stateroom into a hallway filled with the busyness and excitement of a journey about to begin. Everyone was smiling and excited. Old-time passengers knowing the routine, first-timers looking around being guided by crew members of what to do and where to go.

One of the crew stopped him. "Sir, do you need any help knowing where to go?"

Daniel smiled and pointed at his vest we're big black letters have been stenciled on the bright orange jacket DE8. "Staging Area DE8, at the end of the hall, I'd take the stairways down one level and it should be on the starboard side I studied the map on the door of my suite."

"You're correct, sir; not a first-timer, are you?" the crew member said politely.

"No, I think this is my 12th voyage, but it's going to be my longest."
"I think you'll love it. I've made this voyage a couple of times, and it looks like the seas are going to be pretty calm, at least on the first leg of the voyage." The crew member shouted out as Daniel shuffled down the hallway half pushed along by the busyness of the crowd. At the end of the hall, Daniel took the stairs down one level; four crew members were standing in front of the elevators letting folks know that in an emergency the stairs were to be used, more efficient and safer than elevators. At the bottom of the stairs, he smiled at a young lady, a crew member who couldn't have been more than 20.

Just to make conversation, Daniel walked up to and asked the young girl, "Can you tell me where the "Save Us First" staging area is—DE-8?" He knew that was the crew's nickname for the very privileged and wealthy who stayed in the premier suites.

She giggled and pointed. "You're almost there, sir, DE-8 is inside the ballroom at the end of this hall."

"Thank you!"

The door to the ballroom was open and there was one of the crew members standing there with a large sign DE-8. Daniel stood in the general area and made small talk with the other passengers. Angela was standing about 100 feet away, holding a sign DE-7 she smiled at me. I nodded at her. I continued my gaze. Something about her scared me and made me feel comfortable all within the same moment. After about 15 minutes and a few supervisors walking around with clipboards checking things off the all-clear signal was given. An announcement came over the speakers that everyone could go and to have a nice voyage, and the ship would be departing in about half an hour.

Angela walked over to Daniel. "Remember, the captain has invited you to the bridge for departure. Like he said, it would give you a magnificent view of Alcatraz and the Golden Gate Bridge when we go under it. It's truly something not to be missed."

"I'd love to, but I should go put away my clothes."

Angela quickly answered, "I'd be glad to do that for you, sir, leaving the harbor, especially the San Francisco harbor is definitely an amazing sight to see from the perspective of the bridge."

"Okay, thank you, Angela, I'll accept the captain's invitation, but we've got to get this name thing down, it's Daniel, not sir or Mr. Ray, just Daniel. And please leave me a note about what I should be wearing for supper tonight. How about you drop me off at the bridge? I have no idea how to get there."

"I'd be glad to, Daniel, and I won't make that mistake again."

Angela gave her DE-7 sign and Daniel's life vest to a colleague, and she and Daniel wound their way to the bridge. Once inside the bridge, Angela made a graceful exit.

"Mr. Ray, I'm glad to see you accepted my invitation. We are just about ready to get underway," Captain Del Monty said, sticking out his hand to greet his special guest.

"Excuse me for a second!" Captain Del Monty turned to one of his crew. "Let me know when we're free of ropes and ready to go." The captain gave Daniel a quick tour of the bridge while barking out orders.

After a bit the words came. "We're free, Captain, ready to go!" the crewmember said, staring at the monitors.

"Excuse me, Daniel, this is where I earn my keep." The captain went up to the control panel and pushed the lever forward. The sounds of the propeller and its displacement of the water became pronounced, and our journey was underway. With the windows open, you could hear a cheer from the 600 passengers lining the railings. As soon as the ship was in the waters of the harbor, the captain sounded the foghorn, and we slowly picked up speed. Daniel found everything about the experience fascinating. Soon they were passing by Alcatraz. The captain signal Daniel over to where he was standing.

"That's where the guards and the family member stayed Building #64, at any given time there was usually about 300 guards and their families living on the island guarding about 260 prisoners on average. I heard that the food wasn't that bad compared to other penal institutions, but inmates were always cold. The water around the rock was pretty much a constant 51°, something that would be chilling to any man if he tried to escape."

"Any ever make it?

"Yeah, actually two did, but they were quickly rearrested. If I remember correctly, 36 prisoners tried to escape; some were shot and killed, some drowned when making the attempt."

Not much more was said as a captain got busier monitoring their exit from San Francisco.

It wasn't long, and they were getting ready to pass under the Golden Gate Bridge the captain call Daniel over to where he was, "It was never intended to be this color. The steel for the bridge arrived coated in a burnt red and orange shade of primer to protect it from corrosive elements the architect liked the color more than the gray it was to be painted. Thus, the Golden Gate Bridge."

"Interesting!"

"Do you know who H.B. Wobber is?

"No, I can't say that I do."

"He was the first man to commit suicide by jumping off the bridge lesson three months after it was completed. Rumor has it that he turned to his friend as they were walking across the bridge and said to him, "This is where I get off, I'm going to jump." And he did, four seconds later, he hit the water traveling at 75 miles an hour. About 1500 people have killed themselves, jumping off the bridge about one every three weeks. Four seconds that's pretty quick."

Daniel was amazed at the view he was getting enjoying the special treatment that came with being the occupant of the owner suite. He noticed the captain talked less being in his comfort zone, not having to put on a show for his guests. Daniel enjoyed him better. He seemed like a nice man and very competent at what he did.

"Next stop, Hawaii then to Astoria, Oregon then up to British Columbia and Ketchikan, Alaska then we start circling down to Asia." Daniel knew the route and all the stops partly because of his near-perfect photographic memory. Daniel stuck around for about five minutes.

"Captain, thank you for the invite, it was quite delightful something common for you but amazing for me. I'm going to go walk around for a bit then go to my cabin for a little bit of a rest, see you at supper tonight."

The captain who was busy with the many tasks of the departure, waved at Daniel. "Glad you enjoyed it, I always love showing off what she can do. See you tonight at dinner."

Daniel left and roamed the ship eventually, ending up standing at a railing feeling relaxed and grateful to be out at sea again. They were still close enough to land he could enjoy the serenade of seagulls following the ship looking for the fish now closer to the surface because of the churning of propellers. When they were far enough out to sea, Daniel stopped at one of the duty-free stores, bought a box of good Havana cigars, took one out and had the rest delivered to his room. He then went back out to the railing to enjoy it. These voyages were the only place that Daniel allowed himself to smoke for on land ashes from cigarettes or cigar butts always left traces. But here on the ship, he could stand at the railing enjoying a good cigar leaving all traces of it in the ocean. It was one of many small reasons he was fond of these voyages.

After his smoke, he made his way back to his suite. All of his clothes were neatly put away, and Angela had laid out an outfit for dinner on his bed. The box of cigars was placed in the corner of the desk; they must've arrived when Angela was putting away his things. He poured himself a drink went out to the deck area of his suite. He sat there, wondering what the voyage would bring and who would end up dead because of it. He had asked Angela to put together a list of all the upper-tier passengers' something he knew she wasn't to do but also knowing she would. He knew that his next victims' names were on that list somewhere. It was his job to find them. He pondered over the list. He felt some joy and challenge when he noticed Pete Jamerson's name was on the list, even though Angela had told me he was on board. He knew that the poker games would be fun and demand he plays his best. Henry Sanford and his wife, Juliana, the one who fancied himself a poker player but wasn't, they were staying in a suite on the floor below him.

Sanford was all show. He had made a small fortune being the financial backer of a tech quiz and ingenious inventor. The man had been Stanford's lottery ticket. The man invented a tiny switch now used in all computers for it cut down power usage by 25%. It had brought the company that Sanford was the majority shareholder of approximately $150 million and a small percentage royalty that paid the firm about $10 million a year.

Though the inventor was financially secure and didn't care about money, he enjoyed puttering around and using his money to invent more things that added to the world and made Stanford richer, Sanford loved being rich. He always had on his Richard Mille RM011 watch worth a little over $100,000. He always said that he won it in a poker game, but I know his skills are not that good unless he was playing with an idiot, a very rich idiot. But in private, Juliana, after a few cocktails, let me know that he bought it himself. She was a show thing 30 years younger than Henry. There was as much love between them as there was between a wolf and a sheep. But she did look the part, she was stunning and always wearing outfits that showed off her expensive breasts. At the poker games, Henry would talk about how her ass was so tight you could bounce the proverbial quarter off it and what fantastic blow jobs she gave. But I already knew that. On a previous voyage, when I been playing poker with Henry and he got extremely drunk, and I'd won $10,000 off of him, I helped him back to his cabin. Juliana was there and she and me help get Henry to bed. Almost as soon as his head hit the pillow, he was snoring. She asked if I'd like a drink and we just sat down in the living room area of their suite with her husband sleeping and snoring not more than 20 feet away. She looked at me, smiled. "I know my husband always is bragging about my blowjobs at his poker games, would you like one, it'll be our little secret. I smiled. And soon, she was between my legs, showing me what a talented expert she was and what she provided for the marriage. When she finished, she just licked her lips, and helped me do up my pants and sent me on my way

90

with the cute little pat on my ass. She had once again gotten even with her husband. Nothing more was ever said.

There was one other couple on the list who I recognized a Samuel and Charlotte Monterey. I just met them briefly on a short voyage two years ago. Samuel was a man about 70 years old, and Charlotte had been his companion for the last ten years after his wife Mariana had died. Charlotte and Samuel were former high school sweethearts who got together after Mariana's death from cancer. Charlotte had come to the funeral to pay her respects, and old ambers were slowly brought to flame again. I had supper with them one night, and they were delightful. The conversation was interesting, and their respect and care for each other were always present. They were a direct contrast to Henry and Juliana Sanford. They deserved further investigation. I made a mental note to let Angela know I would like to dine with them sometime early in the voyage and to set that up. I then put the list down stared into the blueness of the ocean ahead of me and the sky above me, both fighting for who could put on the most beautiful display. Today it was a tie.

Chapter 14

◆

It had been about three weeks since our group consultation with Bobby's old counselor Jim Syverson. Now once a week, the four of us, Captain Colleen, myself, Alex and Sandy, would get together for two hours going over any new thoughts or information.

Sandy and I, after long hours, put together and plastered on the wall of conference room C a pretty comprehensive timeline. There were known murders in blue. Suspected murders were highlighted in red. Starting with the suspected one in New Smyrna Beach and continuing until the murders of the Deutschs. We now believed that he had been killing for at least 19 years, maybe longer, if our data was correct. There was one three-year break in those 19 years. Those years laid, directly in the middle. Was he in prison, had he changed his MO, or had we just missed some? All of our questions were written down on whiteboard sheets, and hung off to the side.

We were going to start our weekly meeting; Sandy walked in and threw a bunch of files on the table. She was furious. "This is just from one year; there are 323 reports of children having limbs broken by the parents, and this is just in this part of Florida. Some of this shit sickens me. There's a young boy in there pointing at the files age six the police found when responding to a domestic abuse incident, they found him chained to a pole in the attic his bones had been broken in five places." Sandy picked up another file. "Here's one where a young girl had been regularly sexually abused since the age of four. My God since the age of four. Who the fuck would do something like that. Oh, yea, it was her dad, her own father?"

It was cleared to all during these past weeks of reviewing child abuse files that Sandy was losing a lot of innocence having to stare and look at what filthy little creatures and beasts some humans could be. It was rare to see her joyous smile anymore.

Sandy started up again, "And the worst ones are the neglect cases. Did you know the two children from the same family starved to death last year even though the refrigerator and pantry shelves were filled with food? The parents kept their kids locked in the bedroom that they would slide food under the door every now and then. They went on vacation and left the children locked in that room. They said they didn't know what the problem was; they'd left them with a loaf of bread for the week. Well, the children were already sick with diarrhea. Do you know where they're fucking parents had gone? They went to fucking Disney World, fucking Disney World when their kids were starving to death back home. The mother weighed 250 pounds. The sick fuck!"

Bobby had remembered hearing about that case and was glad to see that the parents were put away for 40 years. He secretly believed they should've been left off and left to fend for their own in the middle of the Everglades.

"If this is what creates guys like we're looking for with this shit going on, I'm surprised we don't have serial killers on every block."

Captain Colleen spoke up, "Sandy, I'm sorry that you've got to look at this crap, but someone does, it's the job. Can you take it?"

It was a good question; all of us were wondering the same thing from the look on Sandy's face. There were now tears rushing down her cheeks. She fell into a chair. "I don't know, Captain, I don't know, I walked the streets now staring at people, wondering if they have children wondering what they may be doing to them. I can't get some of these pictures out of my mind."

"I want you to go home, and I don't want you coming back till next Monday. You need to get your head together. Most parents are good, and you're dealing with the worst of the worst" Today was Wednesday.

"First thing you do on Monday when you come in you go see and talk with Margaret Fletcher, the psychologist who works with the police and fire. You're dealing with what we call secondary abuse. You're taking in the children's pain. If you don't set up some boundaries, it will eat you up from the insides out. We'll lose a good cop, and I'm not going to let that happen."

Sandy started to say something. "There will be no discussion, this is an order. I will send you an email of where to meet Margaret on Monday. Now get out of here."

"But Captain, there is so much to do; there is so much to do!" Sandy was now screaming.

Bobby was glad they were back in conference room C, which was quite isolated. He went over to Sandy, pulled her up out of her chair. He put his arms around her, pushed her head on his shoulder.

"Let it go; Sandy, let it go!" She sobbed and pounded on his back. Bobby just kept patting and rubbing her back, telling her to let go. It was something he'd seen his counselor do during his treatment when his roommate was talking about the day as a child he walked into his parents' bedroom and found his mom dead from a meth overdose, she had exploded her heart when he was ten. After about five minutes, much of the agony had drained from Sandy.

"Captain, do you mind if I take Sandy home? I'll stop and get her some takeout and make her eat. I know she won't be feeling like it, but she needs to eat. I'd like to have lunch with her and talk?" Bobby asked.

"You okay with that partner?" Bobby looked at Alex, who was in as much shock as the captain was, having never seen or even believed that Bobby had that much compassion within him.

94

Alex shook his head. "Yes, sounds right to me, partner, sounds right to me."

There was total agreement that that's what would be done; Sandy had no vote in the matter. She just gathered up her files, saying she would work on them at home.

"Leave them there. Alex and I will take care of them." the captain said in her commanding voice. Then her voice softened, you go spend some time talking with Bobby, no work for you until Monday. I don't even want you watching a crime show on TV, just comedies. You ever seen the Big Bang Theory?" Sandy shook her head, no.

"You got Netflix?" The captain asked.

"Yes."

"Good I want you to watch as much as you can from season one on; I'll expect a full report when I see you on Monday after your visit with Margaret."

Bobby smiled, thinking to himself that that would be a good show for her to watch. All the people in it were about her age, and most of them walked around in lots of innocence. Sandy was a bit of a nerd.

They stopped at Sandy's desk and got her purse, and as they walked to the door, Bobby asked, "Do you like Mexican?"

"No, not too much."

"Damn somebody living in Phoenix, and they don't like Mexican."

"I like Thai."

"Good, the only thing I like more than Mexican is good Thai food."

"Ever been to The Golden Orchid?"

"I love that place." There was a small smile on Sandy's face. The first Bobby had seen in a few days.

"Good, we'll stop there and get takeout. I'm going to have their hot spicy chicken and an order of egg rolls."

Sandy laughed. "That's exactly what I was going to have! Maybe we're a lot alike."

Bobby reached over and grabbed her hand and with the compassion of Mother Theresa softly said, "More than you know, Sandy, more than you know."

Somewhere between the egg rolls and the spicy chicken Bobby just said, "My first week as a patrolman, I was called to a scene, and a 16-year-old boy was hanging from a makeshift noose in his garage. I went outside and threw up in the bushes. I can think about him and still see him until this day. I was more upset than his parents. Yes, they were sad, but they kept talking about what an inconvenience this was going to be. Fuck, I had to stand there watching him swing until the coroner and investigative team got there, and we could cut him down listening to his parents talking about this being an inconvenience." He looked up at Sandy tears were running down her face.

"That kid made me a better cop. Six months after that, I was spending time playing with neighborhood kids and other cops in a baseball league that one of the officers had started. By the way, are you any good that baseball you're welcome to be part of our league?"

"I was a damn good softball player in high school; I was a pitcher."

"Good, you're starting next Thursday. Save the date. Sullivan's a lousy pitcher; there's no action on his balls whatsoever."

Sandy feeling a little bit better, jokingly said, "Yea that's what his wife told me at our last picnic." They both just howled. You could feel the tension in the room dropping.

"I agree with the captain I want you going to see that psychologist, Margaret's pretty good!"

Sandy was shocked. "You've talked to her?"

"Yeah, I saw her a bunch of times after treatment. She helped me a lot, figuring out how to be a policeman, a detective doing his job without alcohol, I had to learn how to set boundaries between me, the things I had to investigate, the things I had to stare at when everyone else would look away, and even with me and some of the other cops who didn't know what to do with me since I wasn't drinking. Yes, she's a good woman. She knows a lot of my secrets."

"Like what?"

"That's between Margaret, me and God. Just like yours will be. We should've got more eggrolls. I'm famished."

Chapter 15

———————◆———————

It was the first night of the cruise. I was getting ready for dinner at the captain's table, something I was looking forward to, getting to dine with the Who's Who of the passengers. There was a soft knock on the door, I looked through the little spy hole on the door, and it was my personal attendant, Angela. I smiled to myself. I was glad to see her there's something special about her. She had a humble, unassuming confidence. Even though it was her job to put me first and cater to my needs, I was feeling like I was following, not leading. I open the door and invited her in with a smile.

"I hope you like the outfit that I picked out. I hope I wasn't too presumptuous laying your clothes out on the bed like that."

"No, no, I'm delighted that you did. I see that you also ironed them. Thank you." They shared a smile.

"I liked everything you picked out except for the tie."

She stepped into the suite a couple of feet. "I so agree with you. I didn't like the tie either, but it was the best I could find from what you brought," she said as humbly, then waited to see what my reaction would be. She wanted to know if she had judged me right.

I opened the door of the wardrobe where my ties hung. I could see that from the assortment of ties hanging there, Angela was right. There weren't that many because I don't like wearing ties, but I did know there would be certain occasions like tonight where I would need to wear one. As I was standing there looking at the ties, Angela pulled her hands from behind her back. Draped over her delicate hand was a beautiful tie that would balance perfectly with the jacket and mustard yellow shirt she had picked out.

"Well, there it is, the tie I was looking for, where did I leave it? At the boutique?" I could see the relief on her face I wasn't angry at what she had done. She knew that if she guessed wrong, it could've been a long cold voyage. But she was a good judge of character.

"If you don't like it, I can take it back! Again, I don't want to be presumptuous, but I thought it would go perfectly with the jacket and shirt. There's a small thin streak of blue within it that I think also pulls out the blue in your eyes." I had to admit that she was right.

"It truly is the perfect tie for the outfit. How much was it?" I asked, keeping a pleased tone in my voice.

"It was $200, but I used some of that thousand dollars you gave me to purchase it. As your attendant, I want you to look good; it also reflects on me." I laughed.

"Angela, that thousand dollars was yours, for you; not for you to spend on me. I'm letting you know right now if you need money for things like this or for other attendants to get information for me, just do it. If it's under $500, just spend it, and if it's going to be more, let's talk." I started to reach into my pants for my wallet.

"No, no, consider it my welcome aboard present to you. You're going to be the most handsome man at the captain's table tonight."

I made a face at her. "That's not saying much, I know some of those old coots who will be joining me at the captain's table."

"Speaking of old coots from the tone you used been talking about Mr. Sanford, I seated you next to his wife Juliana instead of him. I hope that's okay." Angelina informed me.

"It's like getting the booby prize, but it will be okay for an evening," I replied.

Angelina looked at me, squinting with a questioning look. "Are you making a joke about her breasts?"

I thought for a second. "Oh, the booby prize remark and the way she shows them off." I laughed. "Oh, I wish I had! That would have been a good one. She's a little bit better than her husband, but not much. And yes, I guess I'll enjoy the view much better than staring at her old husband's snarly old puss. I like subtle beauty, not flamboyant plastic beauty like hers." There was quietness in the room for the words I was saying could have been used to describe Angela. "But please make a note I don't want to be sitting with the Sanfords too much. I think they're kind of boorish and he drinks a lot. Angela, I would like to sit next to Samuel and Charlotte Monterey in the not-too-distant future. I met them once before, they seem pleasant, nice and very interesting, plus they seemed to like each other a lot. I like that in a couple. Henry and Juliana tolerate each other at best."

Angela answered, "The Montereys will be sitting at the same table tonight but not too close to you. Thank you, the things you are teaching me are very helpful. So, your idea of wanting us to get together each afternoon and talk about what will make this a more enjoyable and fruitful voyage is a good one. These are the types of things I need to know."

I added, "Plus, we can talk about my wardrobe and any gossip floating around about others or me." She overlooked my little comment.

"I will get you as much information on Samuel and Charlotte as I can. I'll have that for you for tomorrow afternoon."

"Angela, I want you to know I think our first day together has gone very well, and I'll let the captain know that tonight. Did he picked you to be my attendant?"

"I volunteered; I saw you on another cruise on "The Oceanview" about three years ago. It was a 14-day Mediterranean cruise, and I found you very intriguing, thoughtful, handsome, and exceptionally well mannered. You're much different than the rest of the people who come on these cruises. If it weren't for the suite that you've booked, nobody would know that you're wealthy. I appreciate someone who doesn't wear their wealth and doesn't rub it in other people's faces. I've never liked arrogance, and you don't seem to be. So, when I saw your name, I volunteered to be your attendant. I hope you're okay with that."

I immediately remembered "The Oceanview" cruise.

Audrey and Joseph Fortman had lost their lives and a small part of their fortune because of that cruise. He was a tough old Army man, and Audrey had been his wife of 38 years. All the time he had been in the Army, he had been investing in stocks and was very good at picking them and selling them at the right moment. They were worth several million dollars.

I tasered him and placed him in handcuffs. After he came too, he surmised the situation, thinking it would just be a simple robbery. He started to calculate how to lower his loss. That I was wearing a mask helped take away the fear I would kill them. I opened up my toolkit and showed him the different devices meant to bring pain and humiliation to his wife. He quickly gave up the combination to his safe, thinking he'd be getting by somewhat cheaply. There I found $200,000 in cash.

But on the boat, I had learned the Joseph liked to keep most of his traveling wealth in easily disposable assets. They were simple to hide for travel if needed--his treasure was mainly extremely high-quality diamonds. So, when I only found the $200,000 in cash, I knew there had to be a second safe. And almost always there is. It was when I threatened to humiliate his wife by doing bad things to her. And then slowly pulled up her nightie. He told me about the second safe in the garage. I left their home with $200,000 in cash and close to a million dollars in high-quality diamonds.

101

I placed them in their beds, still zip tied them. Them thinking I would be kind to them, leaving them in a comfortable place until they would be found; at least that was what I was telling them. I still had my mask on. I took it off. They were shocked, recognizing me instantly and also realized what would be happening next. Within seconds Joseph laid there were two bullets in his brain. There were two in Audrey's and a mint on their pillow. I took the zip ties off and left.

I also thought back about the arrogance I had displayed this summer. My breaking my rules. Angela would be good for me, a helpful reminder of how arrogance and prideful ego were dangerous in my line of work. "If you ever see me acting arrogant or treating you as if I'm more special than you, you have permission to call me on it. I was a bit that way this summer, and I'm still mad at myself about it."

"OK, I will, but I don't see you that way." Angela smiled, straightened my tie and then sent me off to dinner at the captain's table, staying behind to tidy up my suite.

When I got to the dining room, I did not need to announce who I was. One of the attendants in white gloves led me to the captain's table and seated me next to Juliana. I was not surprised that she was the first one there. Juliana had on a beautiful sequin dress in many shades of red, and there was her cleavage proud and on display. "Henry is still at the bar, finishing a drink, and e'll be along shortly." Then she leaned over. "Daniel, it's a long voyage. I hope you get him drunk a couple of times and then bring him home. We can put him to bed together as we did before, then maybe you can put me to bed. You got to sample my special talents, but you never really got to meet and enjoy the girls." She glanced down at her breasts. "I think you'd enjoy them."

"You're right. It's a long voyage," is all I said in response to Juliana's offer. I could see Henry walking towards the table with the Montereys to join us.

We all greeted each other. As we were doing that, the three other couples arrived to complete the captain's table. So altogether there were:

The Tiedens--Susan and Paul of Mesa, Arizona, The Dohms--Mikyla and Eugene from San Francisco, California and The Brubakken, Gunvor and Lars from Trondheim, Norway, The Montereys, --Samuel and Charlotte of New Orleans, Louisiana and the Sanfords from North Oaks, Minnesota and myself. As we were greeting each other and making introductions to each other, the captain and the Co-Captain arrived. Henry made some predictable joke about how if the two were here who was steering the boat or was the ship just adrift in the Pacific. The Co-Captain, Magnus Christianson, a younger Norwegian man, made Henry comfortable by laughing at his joke. And informed Henry that yes, during the dinner, the ship would just go around in circles. He then excused himself and talked Norwegian with the Brubakkens. The Brubakkens were immediately scratched off my list. I would not be traveling to rob and murder anyone in Norway, which was where they mostly lived. Though I found out later on the voyage, they also had an apartment in New York City.

The dinner was delightful. I had the escargot, and for my main course, I had simple, elegant, and delicious ratatouille. I limited myself to one glass of wine with my meal, as I always did when cruising. Knowing that I'd be having an after-dinner drink or two depending on how long the card game might go. I saw the Jamersons sitting at another table across the room. I excused myself as we were now having coffee and dessert and said hello. I was genuinely excited to see Pete. It had been about three years, and he was one of the best poker players I had ever played. When I got to the table, I could tell there something was different. Magdalene, his wife, was so glad I had stopped to say hello she took my hand and held it tight with both hands. There was a distance in Pete's eyes. I pulled up a chair and sat and talked for a bit sadly finding out Pete had suffered a stroke a little over a year and a half ago. There was permanent brain damage. He was not the same man. I had so enjoyed him, his quick wit and challenging poker skills, but we all have an expiration date we can't escape, his was getting closer.

Magdalene still holding my hand, "He still likes cruising. At home, he gets easily agitated, and well, he is hard to live with. But when cruising, it relaxes him so. He'll mainly sit out on our balcony or out on the deck and stares out at the ocean. That's why I booked this cruise so that he can have 58 days of some relative peace."

"Magdalene, maybe if you wouldn't mind some afternoons, I could just come to sit with him, have a cigar or cognac and stare at the ocean with him. It's something I enjoy doing myself."

A tear came to Magdalene's eye. "I think he'd like that very much. I know Peter, but also, I would enjoy the company." Daniel had always experienced Magdalene as a very vibrant, sexy, classy woman; the two of them fit well together.

Magdalene patted my hand, still holding it. "Daniel, that's very kind of you to offer." In her eyes, you could see how hard these months had been on her. Pain when it can't be transformed into growth and knowledge or when there is no escaped from it often morphs into suffering. The suffering of the last year was etched into Magdalene's face and eyes. A loneliness was consuming her. It was stealing her personality just as the stroke had destroyed her husband's.

"Magdalene, I enjoyed Pete, his mannerisms, and his skills at poker. He'd give me a damn good run for my money and he took a bunch of it."

"Yes, but I know you took some of his too. He so enjoyed playing against you, but sadly those days are over for him." She hadn't taken her hand off mine. I patted hers. "Life can be so dammed cruel."

I squeezed her hand. "Well, Magdalene, I should be getting back to the captain's table the first night and all, but I'll stop by in a couple of days. Pete, does he still enjoy a good Havanna?"

"That would be nice, but I think he'll mainly just hold the cigar until it burns down."

"Well, we'll give it a try." I leaned over, kissed her on the cheek, and stood up. She smiled and finally let go of my hand, returning into her familiar and ever-constant loneliness.

104

I went back to the captain's table and enjoyed a few minutes of pleasant conversation and subtle flirtation with Juliana Sanford, then excused myself. I wandered the ship, remembering how much I enjoyed this part of my deadly lifestyle. By now, the stars were out. The moon was three-quarters through its waning cycle. It was throwing enough light on the snow-white clouds to illuminate them as they drifted across the ocean--the night sky, how I enjoyed it. I paused and leaned against the railing, took out one of my Havanas I had bought earlier. I relaxed into the moment. No one had any idea of the danger that walked the ship I enjoyed that, my secret.

A young couple in their later twenties walked by, clearly in love, laughing and joking with each other. I would find out later they were on their honeymoon. The couple had gotten married up on Nob Hill in San Francisco the night before. The voyage had been a wedding gift from the groom's family. A wedding was two old money families with each working to outdo each other on wedding gifts.

I was tired—the intensity of the past few months of the hunt and cleaning up after it had exhausted me. I wandered back to my suite. I smiled as I walked in. Angela had laid out my pajamas and left out a bottle of fine cognac, a glass, and there on my pillow was a mint. I picked it up smiled as I unwrapped it and placed it in my mouth. I let it slowly melt from the heat of my mouth, enjoying its sweetness, not like the uneaten mints left on the pillows of those I had murdered now locked away in some evidence room.

Chapter 16

◆

They were all watching Sandy get more jaded as she kept scanning over and reading the files of the children who had to experience things no one ever should have. One day when they had their weekly conference, Sandy blurted out. "Your old counselor friend was right when we find him. We should take him out as we should most of these sons of bitches." Captain Colleen looked over at Sandy as Bobby and Alex looked at each other and raised their eyebrows chuckling.

"What the matter, Sandy? What about due process?" Colleen asked.

Sandy looked at her. "Here's another pair of motherfuckers in our own backyard. I'll due process these two!" She threw the file in the middle of the table.

"He and his wife were foster parents. They started taking care of some foster girls, ages seven and eight. From the report, the wife would get them ready all cleaned up, giving them a nice bath and talking to them about what they're supposed to do. And then she'd send them into the bedroom, and they would sleep with her fucking perverted husband, and he would do every nasty thing you could think of to them." You could see the rage in Sandy's eyes.

"And they walked, they fucking walked, some dumbass clerk put the wrong address on the search warrant instead of 1914 Westwood Lane. Some fucking dyslexic clerk wrote down 1941 Westwood Lane. The cops who had been following the case knew exactly where to go, but the search warrant had the wrong fucking address, and they fucking walked. The girls wouldn't say anything. They had been trained well, but the exam given to both of them showed they were pretty well beat up down there. The parents said that was from the parents that the girls were taken from, not from them. But everybody knew that was bullshit. They wanted the girls back. Thank God, child protection wouldn't give them to them. But here's the kicker. They've had a little girl of their own about four that child protection couldn't take away from them. What the fuck's going to happen to her in a year or two?"

"We can stop by and do a welfare check today," Captain Colleen said, trying to offer Sandy some comfort.

Sandy, almost yelling, said, "No, we can't! No, we can't! Because there were no charges, a month after they were let go, they picked up and left the state. Who knows where the fuck they are now and how many little girls they're destroying? It could've ended right then and there if one of the arresting officers had shot him, saying he pulled a gun on them. That would've been justice."

Bobby piped in. "I know how you feel, sweetie, and you're right, but we don't get to be judge jury and executioner. But you're right."

The kindness in his tone and his words of understanding seemed to comfort Sandy, her rage lessened.

The captain piped up. "Or at least somebody should've shot the fucking clerk!"

Everybody around the table said, "Amen to that!" Each one of them thinking about a resentment they all had about some dirtbag getting to walk because of some lame-ass technicality.

Sandy looked at Captain Donahue, sensing the question even before it was asked, answered in a snarky way, "Yes, I'm continuing to see Margaret, in fact, I see her later today, and yes, it's helping. She reassures me that my feelings are normal. I don't get to act on them. Too bad for that."

Alex threw in, "Well, that's a relief. I'm a bit dyslexic myself, and I was starting to worry that maybe you'd blow me away for my poor spelling."

Bobby threw in, "No, that would be me, Christ. I've always got to check his work. On more than one occasion, my hand was on my trigger." They all laughed.

Alex threw in, "Thank God. You got sober." Capt. Colleen piped up, "Amen to that."

Sandy then spoke up, "All this aside, looking back at all these cases, I've got three young guys I'd like to throw out. The first one is a young boy who put his father into a permanent coma with a piece of a pipe. This after he had beaten him and his mother one too many times, nice going kid-o. The second was some young guy who beat both of his parents up regularly until he was put in juvenile detention. Put him away for good---crazy. He said it was because he didn't like his mother's cooking and because his father was a dick for making him mow the lawn in that way where you get those little light green triangles."

"Yeah, my father always made me mow the lawn that way, it was a pain in the ass, but not were shooting somebody over." Alex threw it.

"The third kid ended up in the system because of the way beat up some neighborhood kids, all of them older and bigger than him because he said they reminded him of his father."

"That alone is not enough for us to give and special attention," Bobby said in a questioning way.

"Yeah, I agree, but when he and his family were being interviewed, they all talked of how afraid they were of him. Sandy started reading from the report. "My kid's crazy, he's fucking crazy, one day I'd given him some well-deserved punishment. He came up and stood in front of me, took a kitchen knife and ran it down his arm cutting it good and told me if I ever touched him again, he'd slit my throat when I slept, and the kid is fucking crazy enough to do it." Sandy looked up at the group. "That's pretty weird, isn't it? And by the way, all three IQs are off the charts, particularly this kid. All three fit the profile that Syverson was laying out to us."

"How bad did he hurt his arm?" Bobby asked

"The file says he put about an 8-inch gash on his arm, used his mother's sewing kit to fix it up himself. He wouldn't let her take him to the emergency room."

"Jesus Christ, that's a tough little motherfucker." Colleen threw in.

"I got a little scared reading the file," Sandy added.

"Any word on where they are now?" Capt. Colleen asked.

"No, I'm not sure at all. I've just been looking over these old cases looking for young guys and gals who might fit the profile. I still got about 35 more to look over. I decided to start with only the ones with extremely high IQs."

Capt. Colleen spoke up. "Narrowed it to just guys. We're all pretty sure, it's a guy, and reading those files about the girls won't do you much good just drive you crazy. And we don't want to be putting any ideas in your head in case you pop." They all laughed and Sandy made a look with her face while pointing at the captain like I'll be going after you first.

"That would probably bring it down to around 20. I can probably have that finished up in a week or week and a half at the most."

"Okay, finish up checking those files out, it'll probably give you a couple more to look at and then let's start putting together what happened to these promising young psychopaths. At least we've got something to work with instead of just sitting here with our thumbs up our butts. Also, look at what happened to their families and family members. I'll get another whiteboard in here where we can start listing these kids and tracking out what happened to them."

All were glad about what Sandy was coming up with. At least it would give them something to investigate. Being detectives with no leads to follow-up on made them feel like fish on dry land. Even though they had other cases, this was the one that consumed them. At least now, even though they all knew they were be drilling some empty well-holes, they had things to investigate.

Chapter 17

◆

We were about two weeks into the cruise. I was enjoying the voyage, especially my afternoon visits with Angela. She was keeping me well informed of what was going on with all of the other high-end passengers. Gunvor and Lars Brubakken were regularly hanging with another Scandinavian couple. Anders and Sophia Magnuson, the four of them, always working out at the gym or sunning themselves poolside. Lars Brubakken was part owner and son of a man who had made his fortune building ships. Angela was putting together little files on all the guests that I was interested in learning about their lives. She was perfect for what I needed.

Hawaii had been fun and after the few days on the ship, it was nice to be on dry land for a while even though I've been there once before I went to see and pay my respects to those who lost their life at Pearl Harbor. It was always amazing how much destruction took place in such a short amount of time.

Angela came with me. She was my own personal tour guide. She seemed to know some of the most interesting details. Like the order of the ships hit, which ones recovered which ones didn't. She laid out all the details in such a manner it was almost like being there that day watching the destruction from afar.

I took her to a nice restaurant before we had to go back on the ship just so I could sit and have an early supper with her and stare at her incredible face. I would just ask her questions, for I enjoyed listening to how she weaved the words together into answers. It was easy to tell she was brilliant; that no detail was too small for her. She wasn't showing off as it was always clear that the information and the conveying of it was more important than her. There was a true humility about her.

Lars Brubakken was worth about fifty million dollars and would be worth many times that once his father passed away, who is in his late 60s. He wasn't a jealous son waiting for his inheritance but very active in the business and would indulge himself and his wife once a year on a high-end cruise. Gunvor Brubakken, she had been a high-end golfer just to stroke or two short I'll being able to get on the tour. She and Lars had met at the oldest and most excellent golf club in Olso --- the Olso Golfklubb. They'd fallen in love basically because of the constant pursuit by Lars of her. He had fallen for her the first time he saw her. With his continuous wooing of Gunvor, he took her away from one of Sweden's most famous golfers, Anders Golson. Now they were pretty much inseparable.

The Tiedens, Susan and Paul were quieter and more subdued both in their early 70s. Every evening before supper, there was a string quartet it played in the vestibule. The two could always be found there, Paul sipping on a whiskey and Susan enjoying a glass of fine wine. Daniel noticed that every morning at breakfast, Paul would be reading some reports. Angela let him know those were reports from his business. He owned a fleet of boats that harvested scallops. "Daniel, each night, the results of each ship's daily caught would be wired over, and his attendant would have them waiting for him at his breakfast table. Him and Susan, our regular cruisers, this is the fourth cruise they've been on this year the other three were two-week cruises in the Mediterranean and Caribbean. Their attendant says that Susan's getting a touch of dementia and Paul keeps pretty good track of her. They had been married for over 40 years. All of this was sounding quite interesting to Daniel; they fitted more the profile of the type he likes to hunt.

"I wonder how much scallop fishing brings in?" he said, wondering out loud.

"I don't know, but I'll check into it for you, one thing that I know is that they're not hurting. All of Susan's clothes, even though a bit common,

112

are high end and their luggage, it's all, Coach. But I'll check on that for you."

She told me that the Sanfords were pretty active and that most evenings, someone or one of the staff would have to bring Henry back to their cabin because of his drinking problem.

"Yea, he's got a pretty bad drinking problem. I had to help him back to his room one night on another voyage after a poker game," I said to Angela.

She looked at me and smiled. "Did you have sex with Mrs. Sanford once you got her husband back to the room, I hear she likes to do that?"

I like the honesty of her question and our relationship so far. "Well, actually, I did twice. Once she just performed oral sex on me, something her husband bragged about and the next time, he just laid there watching it was the least I could do for all the money I took off him that night." Angela just smiled at my honesty somehow; I knew she already knew the answer to the question.

"I hope you use protection; she seems to get around a lot," she said, almost giggling.

"I did. As you probably know, Juliana's nightstand is full of condoms; it's something she demands also. You look a bit jealous."

Angela didn't respond to my statement. She just looked down and blushed. It was the first time I got any clear indication of her attraction to me. She went on.

"The Dohms are living well above their means. Their business is just about to go bust from everything I've read about them in the newspapers and gossip columns."

"He's probably stashed quite a bit of money away in the Cayman Islands, that would be my guess."

113

"That wouldn't surprise me either. They both seem a bit sleazy."

"I agree, and he doesn't play poker; I never trust a rich man who doesn't play poker. Almost always, our male egos demand some type of competition." I was talking with Angela, but my mind was still back on how she hadn't answered my question about being jealous. I liked that.

I was noticing her differently as I entertain the thought she might be attracted to me. Her beautiful black hair hung midway down her back. She had dark almond eyes that were sensual and piercing at the same time. She had delicate lips. But she was taller, and her shoulders were much broader and more robust than that of most Asian women. I had learned, her mother was an "Amerasians," a child born between a Vietnamese woman and an American soldier during the Vietnam war. Angela's mother, Barbara, named after her soldier father's mother, was born in 1966. She was an outcast made fun of for her name and features. She was eight years of age when the conflict ended, and life wasn't pretty for her. Angela talked about the stories of her mother would walk down the streets be called all types of nasty names and have rotten vegetables thrown at her. Angela's grandmother and Barbara finally made it to America in 1984. The next year Barbara met a man through a dating site who got her pregnant. He then backed out of the relationship, and Angela was born being raised by her mother and grandmother. Angela told me she looked more Asian than her mother.

"If I wasn't so tall, I'm sure I could pass as Vietnamese." She lamented.

As she grew up, she became fascinated with her heritage reading everything she could on the Vietnam War and staying current with all things Vietnamese and Asian. She even learned the language. She was Buddhist more because of her culture than any real religious beliefs. "I do like lots of Buddhist tenants, but I don't know if I could practice it as well as I should. I don't know that I could practice any religion as well as I should."

114

She talked for another ten minutes. I was listening, but mainly I was focusing on the way she looked and carried herself. After she left, I went out on my balcony. There was a bit of a chill in the air, for we were now in the Alaskan waters. I saw down on the level below me, Peter sitting in a chair wrapped in a blanket staring out into the ocean. I decided to go down and see him. I grabbed a couple of Havanas, put them in my shirt pocket and headed down to his suite. I knocked on the door, and Magdalene opened the door slightly.

I smiled at her. She seemed a bit surprised. "I thought I'd come and smoke a cigar with Peter and maybe sip some cognac with him."

"Daniel, how sweet it is that you come to be with Peter, but this isn't a good time." I looked at her quite dumbfoundedly and inquisitively. She opened the door. She was standing there wearing a see-through white lace nightgown. I could easily see through it and see her surgically enhanced breasts. They were holding up well. Even at her age, they were sweet and full. She had a friendly triangle turf of dark pubic hair between her legs. I saw some movement and looked past her. There sitting on the bed, was one of the crew in his boxers. I recognized him as a waiter from one of the specialty restaurants. He was Jamaican around 25. She was in her 50s. I must've gotten a look on my face because Magdalene was a tear in her eyes said, "Daniel, please don't judge me, I have needs too, and the doctors tell me there'll be no coming back for Peter."

I compassionately looked at her. "Magdalene, I don't judge you one bit. I would probably be doing the same thing if I was in your spot. The look you see in my face isn't judgment but probably a little bit of jealousy, that young man's pretty dam lucky you're a beautiful woman. You go enjoy him!"

She perked up, winked at me, and jiggled her breasts back-and-forth. "I'm glad to hear you say that. Please know you're welcome here anytime, in fact, if you want to come in, I think I could satisfy both of you. I haven't had a threesome since my college years."

I used my index finger and motioned for her to come closer. I kissed her on the cheek. "Maybe I'll come back some other time. I'm not going to be competing with some 25-year-old stud who's probably hung like a horse." From her reaction, I could tell I was most likely right. "I'm not a group kind of guy."

As seductively as she could, Magdalene said, "Anytime you want, Daniel, just you and me, come on back. But if you won't come in now, I'm going to get back to my friend. I don't want to be rude and leave him sitting there."

Magdalene scampered back to the young waiter leaving the door open. She must have had some exhibitionist tendencies, for soon she was on her knees, reaching inside the young man's boxers, not caring that I was standing there. I could see Peter in the background. He was staring out into the ocean, most likely oblivious to what was going on behind him. I grabbed the door pulled it shut just as I was finding out that my assumptions about the young man were correct. I was smiling to myself but also sad, knowing my old friend was pretty much gone, and life was continuing around him right under his nose. I also knew if I got drunk enough, some night, I'd be banging on Magdalene's door. I always had thought she was a beautiful woman.

Feeling a bit thirsty and sad, I headed down to the bar next to the pool and ordered myself a scotch. Paul Tieden wandered up and ordered a whiskey.

"Paul, how's the trip going so far?" I could tell he couldn't quite remember me. "Daniel, Daniel Ray, captain's table the first night."

The lightbulbs were now going off. "Yes, yes, sorry about that. You're the guy staying in the owner's suite. Good, it's been a pleasant trip, me and Susan are enjoying it quite a bit." I looked at the bartender. "Put his on my tab, and anymore he wants to have this afternoon."

He looked over and could see that Susan was lying comfortably, eyes closed, getting some sun under a warming lamp. "That's quite kind of you, Daniel, mind if I join you?" My offer had the effect I had hoped it would.

"Absolutely, Paul." We shook hands again as he sat down next to me.

We started as guys do. The first thing Paul asked, "So Daniel, what is it that you do?"

"Well, I'm pretty much retired, but I used to run a private hedge fund that did pretty good for myself and my clients. Now I just dabble in stocks on my own and yourself, what do you do?"

"Many years ago, I got into fishing, and after some bad luck and some good luck, I ended up being a Captain of a scallop boat. Now I own eight of them, and I don't do anything anymore except watch over them, which takes me about an hour a day."

"I know nothing about fishing and fish unless it's on the menu and my plate. Is it a pretty good business?"

"Well, it's not fishing, but it gives Susan and me a damn good living."

I raise my scotch glass, "Here's to a damn good living." Paul shot back his whiskey, and I motion for the bartender to fill up his shot glass. Paul smiled. "Again, that's kind of you. He's pouring me a dam good label. This stuff isn't cheap."

"Paul, teach me about scallops and scallop fishing, and it will be worth it. I love learning new things," which was true.

"Harvesting, Daniel harvesting, that's what we call it. That is the first thing I'll teach you."

For the next hour, Paul sat, telling me all about scalloping and running a fleet of ships. I kept motioning for the bartender to fill up his shot glass whenever it would get low. He was a pretty good drinker and could handle it well. I liked that about him.

As a whiskey affected him as I hoped it would, I said to him, "Damn Paul, that's a hell of a lot of work. I hope it's paying you good dividends."

He leaned in. "Daniel, most days it's making me about ten grand a day clear. After paying for the overhead for the boat and giving payments out according to the shares of the guys doing the work, yeah, from the eight boats put together, I clear about ten grand a day."

To help put him at ease about what he had said, I spoke up, "That's not bad, kind of like a nice day with the markets." I wanted him to know we were equals.

"Daniel was the most you've ever made in a day trading?"

"Paul, one day, I made $6 million, but the next day I lost 5 and a half million, but I walked away with a half million for those two days. Not a bad couple of days work."

Paul raised his shot glass. "To a good day's work." Paul noticed that Susan was stirred, so he said he would have to check on her. We shook hands and patted each other on the back. It had been a nice couple of hours. As he was walking away, I said, "Been quite enjoyable, Paul, by the way, do you play poker?"

He smiled. "I love the game I'm making some arrangements for someone to watch over and put Susan to bed a couple of nights a week so I can hit the card room. Will I see you there?"

I raise my glass. "To poker the finest game ever invented. I'll see you there. I end up at the card room maybe three nights a week." I could feel the animal inside of me waking up.

Chapter 18

◆

Two weeks later, at our weekly meeting, Sandy de Cottle announced it she'd finished going over the 20.

"I actually went over all 30 of the cases and I found one girl and two other guys we probably should investigate. She's also extremely high IQ person and remembers all of these are from about 20 years ago. Still, she clearly was a budding psychopath back then. Her brother had pissed her off, so she secretly took the family dog, a German Shepherd who was basically her brother's dog and skinned it, tanned it, something she found out how to do through reading books she had checked out of the library, all the time working with the family looking for the lost dog. Then on his birthday, she gave him a gift box that had the tanned skin of the family dog in it. The report says she smiled at him. "I think it will look great on your wall." The brother ended up going bat shit crazy, ending up in the psych ward for a month. She went into foster care. Jesus Christ, it's your birthday, and you end up in the psych ward because of your psychopathic sister. I'm sure appreciated my siblings a lot more."

Bobby wrote down her name with a Sharpie, and I hung it on the wall with the others. "I can't wait to find out what she's doing now. I hope she's not a veterinarian."

Captain Collen threw in her two cents. "She's either doing 5 to 20 in some State Prison, a politician or working on Wall Street. Those are my guesses." They all laughed and threw out ideas of their own. Sandy, who is getting back a bit of her optimism, said she probably turned it around and was a social worker. Everybody booed that idea, but secretly we're glad to see that the therapy she was having with Margaret seemed to help.

"Okay, Okay," Sandy said, "I really think she's living up in northern Canada killing people and living off their flesh and sleeps under a blanket she's put together with their skin and hair. And yes, I've got an appointment with Margaret tomorrow." It was so nice to see her having some of her sense of humor back even though it she had lost a lot of her innocence. Something they all knew needed to be sacrificed to be in this profession.

Bobby Collins thought she was an international drug dealer going by the name of Sofia. "Hey, that's not fair, that's what I was going to say," Alex piped up.

"Too bad, I spoke up first. You've got to come up with another one."

"Okay, I think she's one of the 20 some presidential candidates we've got running." They all laughed. "No, no, I take that back. I bet she CIA." The room got quiet, all contemplating that he might be right.

Sandy went over the two new guys and their crazy backgrounds and the hideous things they had done to get on this prestigious list they were putting together. Bobby wrote down their names, and Alex hung them on the wall. They all looked at the wall. "Eight budding dangerous young psychopaths, and that's from one-third of the area of Central Florida," Sandy said. There was a quietness as the reality of the odds they in law enforcement were facing set in.

Alex spoke up, trying to lessen the ugly reality they were all contemplating. "Yeah, but you got to remember it's Florida we are talking about, it can't be that bad in Iowa, can it?"

Captain Colleen chuckled, "I grew up in the Midwest. We've got our share of crazies there too. Let's not forget Jeffrey Dahmer the Milwaukee cannibal. In one of the classes I took to put on by the FBI, the guy said that there's probably between 50 and 60 serial killers active at any given time."

120

"Christ, I think that's a gross underestimation from everything I've seen in these files," Sandy despondently said.

The captain spoke up. "Okay! Okay! We all know the odds are against us. But I don't want to go down this road. We're just starting to get Sandy back, and I don't want to lose her again," everyone, including Sandy, laughed, but not the captain. She was dead serious. "So, let's throw the names in a hat and each pick a couple to investigate, and when we get any information, just put it on the wall."

"Cap. You don't need to do this. You've already got so damn much on your plate, let us investigate them. Remember that's what we are--- detectives," Alex, said out loud what everybody was thinking.

"Thank you so very much, but I'm so much into this I've got to have something to do. And you think I'm going to miss some of this fun. Our wall is becoming kind of a strange, sick dating site. "

"Okay, you can pick one but only one, and if we need any help on the others, we'll let you know." That seemed to satisfy her, and they divided up the names. Within a week, four of the names were scratched off. Two were in prison, both doing life for multiple murders. They both had earned that special ranking of a serial killer—one had taken out his entire family. And the second by shooting up the grocery store and killing three people because they had been out of Fruit-Loops. One was dead by his own hand, and the fourth one was actually in the military special forces doing multiple tours in Afghanistan and Iraq.

Nothing could be found on the other four as of yet, including the psychopathic dog skinning little girl and the boy who had taken a knife to his own arm to scare and intimidate his father. The name the captain had pulled out was one of those doing life in prison. Bobby and Alex were glad hers had gotten resolved so quickly. She was always stretched so thin because of her work ethic and because the Chief of Police was always sending her off somewhere to some conference or committee.

Bobby was always confronting her on being a workaholic. Captain Collen's standard response was, "Now get it straight, you're the "holic" I'm co-dependent." He would always shoot back, "You know you can be both." To which she would never respond. Colleen's dream was to be Chief of Police someday, everyone knew that she would be an excellent Chief of Police, but she had two strikes against her. First, she was a woman, and second, she was a smart woman. That scared a lot of people. She always worked twice as hard as anyone else. She was always coming up with new ideas on how to streamline the department procedures. Almost all of them were good.

The Chief of Police, Stan Maysack, was smart and talented, but he was also a good old boy, through and through. He respected Captain Colleen Donahue greatly. He was often stealing her best ideas and making them his own. He was working to keep her down as much as possible, regularly sending her off to conferences, training events, and committees that were meaningless in nature, but where someone's attendance was needed. Stan knew that in a fair and just world, he'd be working for Colleen. But as he always said to his friends, "Thank God life's not fair. If it were, I wouldn't be living in a beautiful home on a lake with my gorgeous younger wife. I'd be living in a trailer park next to a toxic waste dump with an ugly woman with three teeth. Thank God life's not fair."

He was right to say he had done some horrible things as he was growing up through the ranks. It was rumored that he had on more than one occasion while working border patrol before he joined the Phoenix Police Department, he had caught some drug mules taken their product and sold it, left them dead in the desert--treats for the coyotes as they were called. He was one of those cops thankfully, few in number, that if he weren't a cop, those in blue would be hunting him. But since joining the Phoenix Police Department, Stan was squeaky clean mainly because he had enough money stashed away and because he was ambitious and a ruthless politician. He had risen quickly through the ranks and had been made Chief of Police when he was in his mid-50s. But times were changing, and he knew it, but he would make his realm last as long as possible.

It took two more weeks, and another of the young psychopaths have been found. It'd take in some doing. He had smartly gotten married to a wealthy older woman. At the time of their marriage, when names can be changed, he changed his from Steven Colin to Mr. Larry Johnson. She lived three more years dying of natural causes. Larry inherited her small fortune. He had researched her well. She had no children her own wealth had been inherited being the only child of the man who invented how to pump hairspray in aerosol form, receiving pennies from each bottle sold.

She was lonely, quite lonely when she met the young psychopath who made her feel young and vibrant again. Larry was now sailing the Caribbean on his beautiful 35-foot sailboat, always having a crew of two or three beautiful younger women willing to satisfy his needs. But still keeping his eyes out and continuously researching for another rich older woman, preferably with poor health, to seduce and marry. Though he had enough money and was still receiving royalties from the invention that had been his wife's fathers, he, like everyone else, always desired more.

Being an excellent psychopath, he loved a challenge, and finding the perfect older woman to steal from was his specialty. Sandy was so proud that she had tracked him down using her superb computer skills. At the meeting, after Sandy had presented all of her information on Mr. Larry Johnson, it was agreed to scratch him off the list. Though he was clearly a dirtbag, he was a smart dirtbag, and nothing he had done was illegal, sleazy but not illegal. Sandy wanted to send a full report of her findings down to the older woman he was wooing, but the group voted that down deciding to let life and love, even if it's slimy, be what it is, as long as it wasn't illegal.

Chapter 19

◆

I was now playing poker on average about four nights a week. I was glad to see that Paul Tieden had arranged for someone to put his wife to bed and watch over her, allowing him to be a regular member of the group. He was a good poker player. Eugene Dohm from the captain's Table was also a regular player as was a man, Randall Yang of Chinese descent, clearly a man of wealth and privilege.

One night as we were playing, Paul Tieden made a remark that saved his and Susan's life and disappointed me greatly. As a group, we were talking about our mistrust of banks and Paul, who had been quiet piped up, "I love banks. I love their safety. My father was a banker. I keep the lion share of my treasures at my local bank. Of course, I keep a little bit in my safe at home, but that's minimal. If and when I start to run low of these petty cash funds, I just go to the bank and replenish it, very convenient." I was so disappointed to hear this. Paul had been looking like my perfect mark.

Randall Yang's ego started to speak up. "Banks are okay. They fulfill certain functions, but you don't need one if you've got the Titan 1200-XR."

"I agree with you, Randall." I spoke up. "I love the eye recognition feature." Wanting to make it sound like I had one.

"Retinal scanning, that's what the feature is called," Eugene added.

The Titan 1200-XR was an excellent vault, but even with its eye recognition feature, its technology was becoming outdated; there were much better personal vaults. The Titan 1200-XR had its flaws, and I knew every one of them. Besides retinal scanning, you needed to know a combination. The Titan 1200-XR eye recognition feature was somewhat hidden, so thieves unless they knew the model would think it was an ordinary large combination safe. You could give them the combination even show it to them in the manual. They could try all day to open it. Still, it wouldn't work without one first having activated an opening sequence started by the retinal scanning feature. A flaw had been discovered when the thief knowing the system got the combination from the owner, plucked out one of his eyes and held it up to the vault. Soon he was in the safe, taking away its contents. I guess The Titan 1200-XR could recognize terror in its owner's eyes or eye. But no salesman or saleswoman would tell you about this blinding flaw.

"Isn't it great, Eugene piped in.

Suddenly, I was excited again. I had lost one potential mark, but maybe I had gained two.

Eugene asked, "Do you have it programmed to recognize both your and your wife's eyes?"

Randall looked at him as if he was insane. "Are you crazy?" The two men started laughing. Eugene added, "Me neither."

I piped up that I didn't know that it had such a feature, but being a single guy, I wouldn't need it. In reality, I knew it could be programmed to recognize up to three sets of retinas.

Randall added, "Well, I'm married, and I don't need it either." His comment brought another round of laughter from Eugene.

The three of us then discussed and argued with Paul about whether banks were needed. We agreed that they had some purposes, like transferring and holding business accounts. Still, for personal wealth, the three of us argued it was better to keep most of it close to home. As the conversation went on, I kept getting more and more excited, for I knew

125

that both Eugene and Randall lived in different states far away from each other. Randall in California, Eugene in Oklahoma. Eugene brought up the argument that always came up, saying he knew a friend that had lost a lot of his money to crooks who had broken into a bank vault. They popped open safety deposit boxes and took the contents and how because it was a safety deposit box, it was impossible to insure. I know, in reality, these stories were never true. Safety deposit boxes being broken into were more of a myth than any fact. Still, my profession demanded that I help keep the myth alive. So, I said that I also knew somebody who had lost lots of money and jewels to the same type of bank vault robbery. It's got lots of agreement from Eugene and Randell. Eugene was thankful for my comments and support. He gave me a smile and nod of approval.

Paul piped up, "Hello fellas; home invasions are more likely than having safety deposit boxes at banks being broken into." Eugene quickly countered, "If someone broke into my home, then they would have to deal with me and my 38 magnum nobody's getting by me." The way he said it would've made any gun-toting Oklahoman proud. I just raised my glass and said, "Here! Here! To the second amendment."

Little did the two gentlemen know that with each word and phrase they spoke, they were increasing the likelihood of their and their wife's demise. You could see on his face. Paul knew he wasn't going to be winning this argument. Little did he know that he was winning the war. That evening ended with me winning a few thousand dollars from the gentlemen. However, I could've won much more from both Eugene and Randall. Both were mediocre poker players. Paul proved to be as sound of a poker player, as were his ideas about where to keep his monies. I won just enough not to chase any of the players away, knowing that at the next game, I would be losing the money back to them but gaining more information.

The next day as Angela and I sat for our afternoon chat, she told me more about Paul and Susan Tieden. And how much money they were probably making from the scallop harvesting. She had seen the daily sheets he received on how his ships were doing. I listened appropriately.

"That's very interesting. I guess he was telling the truth." I made us both a drink even though she wasn't supposed to drink on duty being the personal attendant for the occupant of the owner's suite has its perks. She liked the Margaritas I would make for her. The secret was high-quality tequila, I used Don Julio 1942 plus lots of lime and salt around the edge of the glass.

"Angela, I'm getting more and more curious about Randall Yang and Eugene Dohm. If you don't have files on them, please make them up." Nothing more needed to be said. I knew that within a day or two, most likely a day, I would know everything there was about the Yangs and the Dohms.

Something interesting was happening. I was starting to feel a bit amorous. I started thinking of going to visit Magdalene or finding Henry Sanford and walking him back to his suite to indulge in some carnal delights with Juliana. Either would've been a sure thing for me. But then suddenly, Angela came to mind. I knew she would say nothing to get in my way, but I knew she would find out for ships are worse than small towns for gossip. I knew her enough by now to know she would be hurt. Was I getting a conscience? The thought scared me but also made me laugh.

Just to make sure I wasn't developing a conscience after we were done. I went down to Magdalene, and Peter's suite and helped move him out onto the balcony. I enjoyed a lustful hour of delights with my old friend's wife, leaving both of us quite satisfied. But it hadn't done any good for as I was leaving Magdalene suite, my thoughts returned to Angela, and I felt bad. I thought to myself, "Shit am I developing a conscience am I falling in love." Then the most dangerous thought of them all went through my head, "Could I have a normal life?" It scared me so much I walk back to Magdalena suite knocked on the door and she answered my knocking with a big smile. I just pushed her in and onto the bed and had sex with her again even though Peter was now in the room.

The next afternoon I was expecting the files on the Yangs and Dohms from Angela. She always got things quicker than expected; that they weren't finished surprise me. She told me the files weren't entirely done; there were some details she was having a hard time finding. She was much quieter that afternoon. By the way, she wasn't saying anything; I knew that she knew about me visiting Magdalene.

I tested the waters. "I went down and saw my old friend Peter yesterday."

"Oh, when was that we all noticed that he spent a considerable amount of time on his balcony yesterday afternoon," she said with a neutral voice.

She had just taught me that all the staff knew that when Peter was on the balcony staring at the sea, Magdalene was in the suite getting her needs met. I don't know why, but the urge came over me, and I blurted it out, "I'm sorry."

Angela quickly said back, "You have nothing to be sorry for, you're on vacation here to enjoy yourself, and she's a beautiful woman." I was getting ready to say something, but I didn't know what to say when Angela added, "But you should know she's becoming quite a bit of a whore. I think it's kind of sad and pathetic for the poor woman. I'm pretty sure it's her way of dealing with her grief and loneliness about losing what I hear was quite a vital man. But not actually losing her husband is making her vulnerable to anyone who wants to use her to satisfy their own lustful needs. But you have nothing to feel sorry about; like I said, you're on vacation and she's a beautiful willing woman. Are you going to revisit your old friend Peter this afternoon or maybe go visit the Sanfords, I hear that they're always up for visitors?"

I had just gotten the nicest scolding I ever had gotten in my life. I knew if I had more of a conscience, I would've felt like a heel, but I just enjoyed the way she was making me feel guilty. And it worked just a bit. It clarified it that she did have feelings for me.

I stood up to go get us a drink and she said, "Thanks. Can I have mine to go? I think I'm going to go read a book on the balcony this afternoon, a little cold but with a good blanket, it would be nice. I bet Peter would like some more time on the balcony." As I walked away, I could hear Angela saying, "Reading a book is good; yes there's nothing wrong with reading." I mixed Angela's drink extra strong I was sure she could use it. I shouted back to her, "I'm sorry, I truly am sorry."

She downed her drink in one swallow and then said, "Good really good as always. Well, I should be going I got some research to do if I want to be able to read that book." It was clear she was proud of herself for the scolding she had given me and that it seemed to have some effect on me. As she was leaving, she put her hand on my shoulder, gave me a smile and gave my shoulder a loving squeeze. "Sir, enjoy your afternoon."

"I will and again, I'm sorry. I didn't know you liked me."

She was about to start her speech again about how I had nothing to be sorry for, but I just raise my hand, letting her know enough was enough.

The next day slipped under my door were two files, one on the Yangs and one on the Dohms. I put them in my safe, for I was taking an excursion that day. The ship made its way down the Aleutian Islands, and we were stopping at Dutch Harbor. After that, we'll be on our way to Japan. I wanted to be by myself. I had thoughts and feelings to sort out. I was also interested in seeing the war museum up there. Dutch Harbor had been the only US territory in North America during World War II that the Japanese bombed and strafed. Though it was only a territory at that time, it was still part of America. The museum was quite interesting. I hadn't known that German prisoners of war were held there and used to maintain the place. They also had an excellent exhibition about the nurses that served on the island. Even one of their uniforms was on display.

I had a nice lunch of turkey, stuffing, mash potatoes, and gravy at one of the local restaurants featuring homestyle cooking. It tasted like a meal one like grandma would have made if one ever knew their grandma, which I didn't. I spent the rest of the afternoon walking around the island, enjoying its Spartan landscape, not returning to the ship until about 15 minutes before it was about to depart.

I didn't see Angela the rest of that day or the next. I stayed in my room having my meals, except for breakfast, studying and going over the files she had put together on the Yangs and Dohms. The information from the files and what I was learning at the poker games I was getting a good picture up both the Yangs and Dohms. They continue to look like good prospects.

Eugene Dohm owned a chain of quite profitable car dealerships throughout Oklahoma. He had started working at a dealership not going well because the owner was a horrible businessman. Its' true potential just screamed at Eugene. He did everything he could to scrape up the money and bought the dealership from his boss. Within a year, he had turned it around and was starting up another. Mikyla was a fiery Greek woman who he'd use in some of his TV ads that was both funny and sensual at the same time. He fell in love with her, and they married. He also was featured in the ads. He would be sweeping the car lot as Mikyla was selling the merits I've why people should shop at the Dohm's Chevy store. At the end of the commercial, she would always point to the man sweeping the car lot or doing some other menial job. "Oh, by the way, that's my husband come in and talk to him I'm sure he'll give you a good deal. Just tell him you're a friend of Mikyla." Then she would look sexy and wink at the camera. Eugene talked about how their clever advertisements had built a name and a loyal customer base for them. Because they were in the ads, it was also pretty cheap for them to make them. They would put out new ads every few months people were always looking forward to them. Everyone had their own favorite.

As they arrived in their mid-60s, Eugene packaged all the dealerships together and sold them to a large consortium. He and Mikyla were worth tens of millions of dollars, so he said. Angela, being an excellent researcher, found out that they got $150 million in the deal. Eugene had played down how much they had made, as any good car salesman would do. They now live in the countryside outside of Oklahoma City, not far from their country club. Eugene would play golf almost every day when they were not cruising. Mikyla had become quite the socialite in their area on lots of committees and doing lots of good deeds. She exercised daily, keeping herself in good shape and looking dam good for being 67.

It was clear they were in love from the comments that Eugene would make about his wife during serious moments in the poker games, which there were always a few of. Plus, Angela had put in her file that the staff enjoyed them a lot. They could regularly be heard at night, being amorous with each other. Angela said it was nice to see a couple their age still madly in love with each other. They had had two children, a boy, and a girl now both grown up with families of their own. Neither of them had wanted to be in the family business. But both got some seed money to start businesses of their own, which were doing fine. The Dohms had three grandchildren they often visited and indulged. Eugene told me during one of our poker games how, when his grandson Billy was turning three. He had given him a fully functional miniature Chev car. It worked like a golf cart. It had lights and a horn that played the tune of the Oklahoma Sooners when pressed. "It was a write off we used it in many of our ads, everyone loved the horn."

Yang's were a different story. Randall owned an import and export company that did exceptionally well based out of San Francisco. He was always branching out with his latest adventure. Randell had bought an oil tanker and was renting it out surprisingly, making good money. He was the type of man always doing some kind of deal. Even on the ship, most of his day was spent in the business center. He got up early, had breakfast in the main dining room his trophy wife slept in and had breakfast delivered to her in their suite. He and his wife would have lunch together in the main dining room. The afternoon would be spent with them around the pool, with his gold chains hanging around his neck often on his phone. If he had work to do, Ivana would hang around the pool wearing her skimpy shiny bikinis, always a different one each day.

It was clear they didn't like each other that much. Ivana was gorgeous, that was her job. In public, she had two jobs to be beautiful and to doubt all over him. While he was doing his business dealings in the morning, she would always work out or getting treatments at the ship's spa. Even at her

131

age in the mid 50s, she could be mistaken for a model. But again, that was her job to look good for him. But Angela let me know theirs was one of the few suites on the ship that had twin double beds instead of one large queen-size bed or a king-size bed like in the owner's suite. When the ship would dock, she would always go out shopping, and he would stay in the business center and then meet her for lunch. She would buy two or three stylish outfits that after she wore once or twice, she would have them packaged up. An attendant would mail them to their house in the hills outside of San Francisco at the next port of call. His job was to make money. Hers was to look good and spend his money. Both were good at what they did.

Randall said that they had met when he was over in Russia on a business deal. It was clear that he probably purchased her exchanging a life of luxury for whatever she did for him, which I'm sure was not fun for her, for he was quite fat and gross. Angela always said the thought of having somebody like him crawling all over you was repulsive, and I'm sure it was for his wife. They were the type of folks that if and when I took them down, I would find pleasure in doing it, and they would probably find relief from their charade of a life.

Chapter 20

◆

I wasn't visiting Magdalene anymore. After a few more days, everything was back to normal with Angela and me. As we were heading over to the Japanese Islands where we would have a few days at different ports of call, I got a call from Angela right around the time we were supposed to meet. "Daniel, I can't meet with you today something's come up; I'm not feeling well." I could tell something was wrong by her tone of voice. Also, she was giving me contradictory messages, saying something has come up, and then saying she wasn't feeling well. I knew when someone was lying, especially someone who wasn't very good at it, but I would not press it.

"I hope you feel better let me know if we can meet tomorrow." I knew something had to be quite wrong because that night, someone else turned down my bed and put the mint on my pillow. I made sure to be there when the person came to turn down my bed. "Is Angela okay?

The woman would not give me any information, even if she knew. I kept pressing and put down two hundred dollars. "Sir, I'm not sure all I know is that she's been in her room all day and that she's been crying. Maybe she got some bad news from back home that happens sometimes. We're all away from our homes for long stretches. Almost always on the cruise of this length, someone gets some bad news from back home. Maybe it was her turn." That helped put my mind to ease, it made sense, but it was just the woman's guess.

I was feeling powerless and needed to do something. I went up to the specialty restaurant, for I knew that Angela loved Italian food. She had told me this, and whenever I dined there, she would ask me about my meal and what I had, making me tell her about it in great detail. They weren't allowed to eat at those specialty restaurants. The crew had separate dining areas. Angela told me the food was good but not like the gourmet food at the restaurants. I went in and talk to the Head Chef, asking him to put together a fantastic meal and then told him to have it delivered to Angela's living quarters. He was a bit reluctant, saying he could get in trouble, but two one-hundred-dollar bills dissolved his reluctance rapidly.

The next day at our regular time to meet, instead of coming in, there was a knock on the door, and Angela waited until I answered it before coming in. She looked pale, and her eyes were red as if she had been crying. Angela was wondering if it would be okay if we didn't meet that day; she had a lot on her mind. I notice she was also wearing a scarf around her neck. I told her that would be okay, but I wanted her first to come in and sit down and tell me what was going on. I fixed myself a Scotch on the rocks and an especially alcohol-laden Margarita for her. We sat on the balcony staring out into the ocean. I was waiting for her to take the lead. What the woman the night before had told me about getting bad news from home kept going through my head.

Finally, in as caring a voice as I could, I asked, "Did you get some bad news; is everything okay back at home with your mother and grandmother I know she's old."

Angela, weeping softly said, "No, Daniel, everything is fine back home. Everything is fine. My problem is here."

Being self-centered, I immediately said, "I haven't done anything to upset you, have I? I know I haven't visited Magdalene anymore since our talk."

That brought a soft chuckle to her; she put her hand on mine. "Daniel, it's nothing you've done, you've been purely wonderful to me." She reached up and took off the scarf, and her neck was red. I instantly recognized the marks; someone had tried to choke her.

"Who was it? What did he do?" Everything inside of me was enraged, but outwardly I was calm, staying sympathetic. Something that hadn't happened in years happened. The scar on my arm started to hurt. "Did he...."

Angela interrupted me before I could get the word rape out. "No, no, he wasn't successful. But he tried he held me up against the wall in his room he had asked me to help him carry something in there and stupidly I did. He held me up against the wall with his hand around my neck, and he tried to tear off my pants. But Daniel he touched me, he touched me in my sacred place before I was able to knee him and hit him in the forehead with something heavy that I found on his shelf. I ran out of his room and got back to mine. No one's ever done that before to me. No one's ever tried to take me. It was horrible." Her weeping was steady now. I move closer and put my arm around her. She jumped a bit. "I'm sorry, I'm sorry." I pulled my arm back.

"No, it's okay. I'm just a bit jumpy please if you wouldn't mind put your arm back, it felt nice, I felt safe." I did. I liked holding her.

"Have you turned him in; he needs to be dealt with I'm sure. They'll kick him off the ship at the next port of call."

Almost frantically, she said, "No! No! Daniel, I can't do that. That's not how it works here. When things like this happen on these ships, and there's no proof. We'll both be let off of at the next port of call. It just gets too messy for the company, especially when it's he said she said type of thing like this would be. No! No! I just have to stay away from him.

Being a bit naïve, I said, "But there's proof he's got to have a mark on his forehead and your neck."

"Oh, he does, I hit him good, but he'll just say that he forgot to duck and hit it on one of the steel beams in our living area. No! No! Everything will be okay. I'll just stay away from him. It's so nice to be able to tell someone I couldn't tell anyone in fear of the company find it out and letting me go."

135

I could tell she was calming down just by us talking. I fixed her another strong margarita. We just sat with my arm around her as she wept at the near loss of her innocence. She kept talking about how nobody had ever tried to do that to her before. "Of course, I'm not a virgin, but it's so different when someone wants to take you without your permission. I feel so bad he touched my womanhood, and it wasn't his to touch."

I told her I would call up to the Italian restaurant and have them send down some food for us. I wanted her to stay for a bit.

"Oh, shit, I forgot to thank you for sending me that food last night, oh my god, how selfish of me not to thank you; it was delicious. I should've called and thank you right away." It was the first time I was getting to see a bit of her back.

"How about we have the same thing tonight I had them fix last night. They made it especially for you. I told the Chef you were sick and that you were the best personal attendant I'd ever had. He told me he could get in trouble, but I convinced him. I hope you enjoyed it."

"Oh my god, when I saw it, I knew where it came from, and it was the first time yesterday I felt okay and safe. Plus, it was absolutely delicious! Oh my God, the sauce." I smiled, seeing her excited again.

I picked up the phone and called the restaurant and asked for the Head Chef. When they put him on the line, I told him to fix the same thing he had the night before, but for two and send it to my room, I would be dining in with a friend.

I reassured Angela that everything would be okay, knowing it was. She would be feeling safe again. Angela made me promise not to tell anyone. I squeezed her shoulder. "Don't worry, I won't be telling anyone, and everything's going to be okay, I promise."

Shortly afterward, the food arrived. We had a delightful evening eating fantastic gourmet food and pushing the ugliness of what had

136

happened out of her mind at least for a while. When she had to leave, I stopped one of the older female attendants walking down the hall. I ask her to escort Angela back to her quarters, telling her that Angela wasn't feeling well. The woman reassured me she would get Angela safely back to her quarters. I went back into my suite, poured myself a tumbler of whiskey. I went back out onto my balcony, standing there staring out into the sea, feeling a rage boiling inside of me rubbing my scar. I would be sharpening my rage into a tool to do what needed to be done.

Chapter 21

◆

Nothing much was happening in terms of the case. In the past week, we had had two murders, both related to drugs, part of the chaos being created as gangs fought over the routes coming up from the border. We had solved both quickly from tips on our hotline. People could get $1000 and remain anonymous if a tip led to us solving the crime. The tip line gave us many crummy leads but also some very productive ones. This week had been a good week, a very good week.

I was regularly courting Kay, as Jim had recommended. Everything was going fine. We had progressed to the point now after date night she would let me come into the house, tuck Joey into bed and we'd sit on the couch talking and even make out a bit. I felt like a 17-year-old kid again; only I had an eight-year-old son in the next room. I think Kay appreciated and enjoyed how slowly we were taking it. She got to be in control, real control for a change. There was one date night when we were making out on the couch, Kay let me reach inside her blouse, touch and play with her breast. She reached down, felt my excitement, and stopped us.

She walked me to the door, smiling. "I'm sending you home with a raging boner. Good luck! You deserve this for all the frustration you've put me through."

Laughing, I said, "Still working out some issues, are we?"

"Oh, I've got issues, honey, lots of issues. Some of them go back to before you were drinking; hell, some of them even go back to before I knew you. All that repressed Catholic shame, I've decided to let it all go. Time to deal with it all. Time to drop the rocks and get back to living.

We're going to have fun working them out, or at least I am." She was exciting and scaring me all at the same time.

She gave me a big kiss, grabbed my hardness gave it a squeeze, and sent me on my way. I think I was enjoying this courting more than she was. I was enjoying her newfound strength and confidence. It was looking good on her. My drinking years had been hard on her psyche; she didn't have drunken fog to run into and hide within like I did. She had to stare directly into all the ugliness that my illness was creating. We had stopped living and were working just to survive. It had stolen much of her playfulness, which had always been an enjoyable part of her. It was so nice to see it returning. She was right; it was time to get back to living, but this time I'd be following her lead.

On our next date night, we were sitting on the couch talking. I was secretly wondering and hoping that we would get to fool around again, maybe even take it a bit further this time. I might get to second or even third base? God, I was feeling like and even thinking like an adolescent boy again. When Kay said, "Have you got any vacation time saved up?" I was stunned by her question. "Yeah, I've got about a month, and even more if I add in the comp time I have coming, why? Do you think the three of us are ready to go on vacation?"

In a voice I hadn't heard in years, she said, "I thought that maybe you and I could go away for a bit. I know I can get someone to watch Joey. I think he would be supportive. You know how kids always want their parents back together. He is doing so much better around the house and in school since we have been dating." I made a mental note: SEND JIM SYVERSON A THANK YOU CARD AND THE GIFT CERTIFICATE TO THE BEST RESTAURANT IN MINNEAPOLIS.

For a second there, I was speechless tongue-tied. "Do you think we're ready? I mean, well, do you think we're ready, I mean ready?" I think she enjoyed the fear in my voice.

She grabbed my hand, rubbing it in a way she hadn't done in years, softly and sweetly, she answered, "I think so. I know I am, and I know I want to. How about you?"

I couldn't help myself; my emotional dam broke. I cried, hysterically crying. I had been so afraid this day would never come. Part of me had resolved to love her from afar. She was telling me there was hope more than that even, she wanted me back. Kay pulled me to her, holding me against her breast comforting me like I had seen her comfort Joey during my drinking days when I was in a drunken haze, and he was scared. I cried out, "I'm so sorry, honey, I'm so sorry for what I put you and Joey through. I don't deserve you. I don't deserve you."

She rubbed my head. "It wasn't your fault Bobby, it was your disease. And if you remember, I wasn't that great either I think I'm getting ready to let you come home. Maybe we deserve each other."

I hadn't cried this hard since treatment. After family week up at Hazelden, I had once cried like this. But I didn't do it in front of Kay and Joey. But cowardly in my room in the middle of the night, my tears being soaked up by my pillow.

We stayed like this for about a half an hour, then Kay said, "Bobby, let's go away together just you and me."

"Anywhere you want, honey, anywhere you want."

"Really anywhere?"

"Anywhere!"

She sat up. "You know I've always wanted to take a Caribbean cruise, could we do that? I know you hate cruises."

"Absolutely on both counts. We can do that. I've never been on a cruise, so how could I have an honest opinion. In the program, we would call that "contempt before investigation." and what type of detective would I be if I wasn't willing to investigate and let the evidence make the decision. Kay was so excited that she started unbuttoning her blouse, but then she stopped and buttoned it up again. "No! No! we'll save that for the cruise."

I laughed. "Still working out some issues, are we?"

"Oh honey, I guarantee you we'll work out a lot of issues on the cruise. We may never leave the room, you know it's been just as long for me as it has been for you and you remember how I can get."

I was tired from all the emotions. "Sweetie, I'm going to go back to my apartment now. I think those are some good memories to send me home with."

She had a twinkle in her eyes. "Yeah, those are good memories; I know what I'll be doing tonight."

I was startled thinking about what she was hinting at. "You?"

"Of course, honey, of course! What do you think I do after date night, maybe on the cruise I'll let you watch."? Then instead of saying goodbye at the door, she walked me to my car, we kissed good night. As I got in my car, she said she'd research cruises.

I was so exhausted that as soon as I got back to my apartment, I laid down on the bed, reflecting on the night and immediately fell asleep. Waking up the next morning, fully dressed when the alarm went off. I called Alex for we would get together in about half an hour. I told him what had happened with Kay the night before and how I had just woken up. I told him I needed a shower and a change of clothes. He was happy for me. He suggested we meet at the Old Southwest Diner on Canal Street in about an hour and a half for breakfast. That sounded wonderful. I was famished.

Chapter 22

━━━━━━━━━━ ◆ ━━━━━━━━━━

The next couple of days, I was keeping an eye out, looking at all the staff. One day while walking down the hall, I saw a man with a handful of towels. He must've been in his 40s, muscular with a hell of a bruise on his forehead. I blurted out, "My god, that must have hurt. How the hell did you get that?"

"Yeah, it still hurts, and it was a couple of days ago. I rammed my head into one of those steel beams. Our living quarters can get quite tight." I instantaneously knew this was the man who had accosted Angela.

"Heal well, young man, heal well and remember to duck." Those were the only words we spoke. But I knew who he was and immediately memorized his face and features. I figured he was 5 foot 10, about 180 pounds worked out. His complexion was naturally tan. He had dark hair probably came from a mid-eastern country, maybe Iraq or Iran. There were a few guys from those countries working on the ship sending their money home. As I watched him walk away, I notice he had a little bit of the gait favoring his right side. My information gathering about him had begun.

After a couple more days of us talking, or more accurately, me listening as Angela sorted things out things. We were getting back to normal, but she still startled easily. "Daniel, why would someone want to take something so special to a woman something that always should be given, not taken? Hell, there's plenty of women crew or passengers on the ship who would have gladly given him what he wanted. He's good looking enough that Magdalene would've let him visit her room. Taking a small,

142

deserved shot at me. The crew is always finding passengers wanting a little fling with someone of a different nationality or race."

"Do you know where he's from?" My curious nature asked.

"Iran, with their economy, the sanctions and everything, lots of people leave Iran in search of employment. We've got about 20 people from there working on the ship. Most of them are wonderful people but keep to themselves." It was nice to see she could now talk about him without tearing up or her voice cracking.

I was casually following Angela's would-be rapist, without being noticed, one of my specialties, learning his routines and mannerisms.

Our next port of call was Tokyo. We would be there for two days. It would happen there. I wanted things taken care of, so Angela would feel safe again. I would take a life but not out of greed this time. I would be an agent of justice. I convince myself with little effort that if he had tried this with Angela, he most likely had with other women and had gotten away with it. I despised those types of men. They reminded me of my foster father and my first kill. Men who picked on what they thought were weaker people. The butcher knife and Angela's knee let two know they had chosen wrong.

I told Angela I would be busy both days in Tokyo. So, we wouldn't be able to have our regular meetings about what was happening on the ship. She understood, also letting me know that most of the crew was getting time off each day for a little R&R. She had never been to Tokyo. She was going to explore it with a couple of her girlfriends from the ship. She said she was going to ask me if I would be OK with us not meeting. So, everything would work out perfectly. I was so glad to see she was healing enough to want to venture out instead of staying locked safely in her room. I was amazed at how resilient she was. I gave her $300. "Buy yourself something special." She looked at me. "Thank you, but this is too much." She gave me $200 back. "With $100, I can buy myself something very special. Daniel, you should be more frugal with your money." I laughed.

Then I had a memory from back in the days when I was in the foster homes. Little Rita O'Donald, a freckly red-haired girl of Irish descent, was in the same sick foster home I stayed in the longest. She would be used by both the father and mother regularly. From the sounds coming from the bedroom, things were not pretty. But always the next morning, Rita would be up and about as if nothing had happened. Sometimes with bruises all over her. She would then go out into the world, stealing and robbing folks saving up the money. She never went to school. One day I came back to the house, and there was an ambulance taking away my foster mom. Rita had stabbed her in the gut and was gone. My foster mother recovered, but I never saw Rita again until two years later. I ran into her coming out of the store. She was looking good. She saw me she ran over and hugged me and we went over to McDonald's, got something to eat and talked.

Her first question was, "Did the old fat bitch make it?"

I told her she did, but I'm sure she had a nice scar.

I asked her what happened in those nights. "Oh, those days are gone, I guess you could say I was getting an education about the world from those two. But those days are gone, and I'm doing okay. I've got a sugar daddy who, even though I'm only 16, has got me a lovely apartment and gives me good spending money. He doesn't come over that often, but I don't mind it when he does. It's not a bad job. I got my GED, and he says he'll pay for me to go to college. All I have to do is do those things that he likes, and he is not that kinky, just lonely, and because of that, we understand each other pretty well." He's better than they were a hell of a lot better. After we were done having lunch, I asked if I could see her again, for I had always liked talking to her.

She just looked at me, "No, I don't think so, those days are over with and sorry to say you were part of them, a good part, but still part of them. I don't like to carry things forward. I hope you can understand it's nothing personal." I nodded that I did. She patted me on the cheek, turned and walked away, and that was the last I ever saw of her. It was a pleasant memory. I'm sure she is still doing well. I would bet she got her college degree and has left all of that behind her. Angela's resiliency had reminded me of Rita.

When we arrived in Tokyo, I spent the first day looking for a spot. I knew what I needed and scoured the city looking for the perfect place to do justice. I found it in the Asakusa district of Tokyo. It was an area that wasn't busy except for around the Senso-ji Temple. The community was considered pure Shitamachi (Old Tokyo). There were small alleyways where I could place myself. Almost as if it was meant to be, there was a tiny dress shop a couple of doors down from the alley I had chosen. Everything was perfect. That night I got back to the ship, and I found Angela's would-be rapist and took him aside.

"Are you off tomorrow?" I asked, already knowing the answer. He nodded his head, yes. "Would you do me a favor it's a big favor no it's a huge favor, I'll give you $500. But you have to be discreet, very discreet. It shouldn't take you too long." His eyes and ears perked up.

"Absolutely, sir, what is it?"

"Well, I'm a bit embarrassed, but there's a little dress shop over in the Asakusa district of Tokyo. Well, I had something made for a woman friend of mine on the ship, a special little outfit. It's kind of naughty, that's why I need discretion. I would pick it up if I could. I have to be somewhere else."

He smiled. "I understand sir, I understand and your secret will be safe with me."

"Good, my friend Magdalene it's going to love the outfit. It's made of leather."

By the massive smile on his face, it was all coming together and making sense to him. I was counting on him knowing Magdalene's reputation, and it was clear he did. Someone like him would always be caught up on the sexual gossip of the ship.

"The schedule is a little bit tight. The owner said that the dress would be ready at 12:15, but their shop closes at one." I had chosen this time because the shop actually closed at noon.

"Sir, I'll be there right at 12:15. I hope you don't mind if I spend the rest of the day enjoying Tokyo; you probably won't need the dress until that evening anyway," I told him that would be fine. I gave him a slip of paper with the address of the store and $100. "I'll give you the rest when you give me the dress. I'm stopping at a bank to get some more cash had a bad night at the poker table. Also, let me know if I owe you anything for taxis or subways. This will be $500 clear for you."

"I understand, I totally understand. Thank you for choosing me."

"No problem, a friend of mine told me you would be perfect for the job. A man of discretion."

"Who was that?"

"Discretion, young man, discretion." We smiled.

As he was walking away, I added, "It's nice to see that that bruise on your head, it's almost healed, it looked quite nasty."

"It was sir it was. But I'm going to be more careful next time I get near that beam."

The next day I was up and in the city, early. I found the clothing store where I could find an outfit that looked very vanilla and would fit over mine. I bought one of the local hats that covered me in my face well. Though there were a lot of cameras as I walked around, I practiced noticing them and hiding from them. I had already seen there were fewer cameras in the alley, partly why I had chosen it.

At precisely 12:05, I was in the alley smoking a cigarette to the one camera positioned in the alley. I would look like some man stopping for

146

a smoke. At precisely 12:10, I saw Angela's tormentor walking towards the shop in the reflection of the small mirror I had placed up against a streetlight. As he reached the alley, I stepped out into the blind spot where I would not be seen by the camera. I grabbed his arm with one arm and pulled him nearer to me. In my other hand, I was holding a 9-inch half-inch thick spike with the small t-shaped handle that fit perfectly in my hand. I had had a half dozen of these killing machines made for me. There was a little pressure button on the handle that, when pressed with my palm, six half-inch barbs would pop out of the sides of the spike. I thrust the spike in his ear, seeing the other end coming out of the other side. I press the button I could feel the barbs being released I twisted the handle a few times, knowing what I was doing to his brain. He dropped to the ground, motionless, a tiny trickle of blood ran down from his ear onto his cheek. I put my rubber covered fingers to his neck, and there was no pulse. I went through his pockets, finding the piece of paper with the address of the store on it, which I took. I also took all his money, leaving his pockets turned out and his billfold on the ground I grabbed the mirror and walked away. I got my $100 back plus interest. I left the spike embedded in his brain; they would have to dig it out. I looked at my watch. It was 12:12. I was always amazed by how quickly death could arrive.

From my walk the day before, I knew where there was another alley two blocks away that I could pop in to, and there would be no surveillance. There I took off the outer set of clothes I had been wearing for the kill, placed them into a shopping bag but leaving the hat on and left. The day before, I have seen a Red Cross donation box on the route back to the ship. I was glad for the excellent work and proud of the Red Cross, for they had originated in the state where I was born. It was good to see that they were all over the world doing good. I made my donation I threw the bag with the slightly used clothes into the bin and walked on. As I got back to an area where it would've been more appropriate for me to have walked to from the ship to do some shopping, I casually took off the hat and did a bit of window shopping. I stopped into a store I'd seen from the day before and made a small purchase. Outside, a man was begging on the sidewalk, I gave him $20 and the hat. He smiled, put the hat on, and bowed multiple times towards me. I bowed back. I was back at the ship sitting in the main dining room with Paul and Susan Tieden by

1 o'clock, having lunch. Not more than an hour ago, I was taking a man's life, and now I was engaged in small talk about what we had seen and bought during the Tokyo stopover. Susan asked if I had bought anything. I smiled. I opened the bag at my feet. I took out a high-end French Lieutenant blue golf shirt with the name of the company that had made it discreetly embroidered above the pocket—it said, Justice.

Susan remarked that she had heard about that brand and that it was known for its excellent quality, saying it should hold up well. I've had seen it the day before as I was doing my walking tour of Tokyo and I bought two. One for myself and a lady's version for Angela.

The ship was to depart at 5 o'clock, and there was an announcement that the ship would not be leaving until 5:30. They were waiting for a crewmember who was late. I knew the captain could wait until midnight of the next month, and his crew member wouldn't be coming back. At precisely 5:30 PM, the ship pulled out of port, and we were on our way.

The next day Angela came into my suite all happy and relaxed. I was sitting on the balcony going over the files making some notes. I kept the records in my safe, and as soon as there was no need for them, I took them to the business office area and personally put them in the shredder. I had only two files left, one on the Dohms and the other on the Yangs. Angela was all smiley singing a soft tune to herself, one I couldn't recognize. She was gathering up my clothes to send to the ship's laundry, and then she sat and set about polishing my shoes. I asked her what the song was.

"I don't know the name of it. It's a child's lullaby in Vietnamese that my grandmother used to sing to me before I went to bed."

"It's nice, and please sing it louder." It was a beautiful tune, and she had a beautiful voice. I was curious what the song was about it was so relaxing and peaceful. "Do you have any idea what it is about. It sounds like it's telling a story."

148

"My grandmother told me that It's about a small child who gets lost in the woods. Her grandmother finds her and carries her back to their home and puts her to bed." I don't know if it's a real song or if my grandmother made it up, she was clever like that, but I like it.

"Me too." It felt peacefully pleasant her working in the other room singing and me out on the balcony reading, studying, and watching the ocean.

"Aren't you wondering why I am so happy today."

"No, I'm just enjoying it."

"The crew member who didn't make it back to the boat before we left—well, he was the man who tried to take me."

"That's a bit strange, don't you think?"

"I think he was worried that somehow the company had found out, and he believed he was going to get throwing off the boat or go to jail, so I think he got scared and ran."

"You're probably right." I said, staring at her beautiful smile. "Yes, you're probably right, those types of guys are always cowards at their core." Secretly I know that those types of men never run. They have an entitlement about them and a sense of arrogance, always believing they will get away with what they do. "Please sing that melody again. I like it." Those were the most peaceful soul-soothing moments I could ever remember. I wished that time could stand still and that I could capture this moment forever. I knew I was in love.

149

Chapter 23

◆

We were no closer to finding the identities of the three psychopathic youth, and it was upsetting to all except for me. I was on cloud nine because of how Kay and I were doing. Almost every night when I had a chance, I was eating supper at the house with her and Joey. We were acting like a family again. Joey showed me his report card. He had improved a full letter grade. Kay and I looked at each other, knowing this was what recovery was all about.

I made him tell me the story of how and what he did to improve in each subject. "You know, Dad. It's not that hard when you go and talk with the teachers and tell them where you're having a problem. They're really helpful. They have helped me figure out a lot of things I didn't understand, especially with math."

His mother, who was doing the dishes, said, "Amen to that!" She toweled off her hands, came and stood behind him, and listen as he and I talked about his improvements. She bent over and kissed him on the top of his head. "My boys! My boys!

"Joey, I want to let you know something, Dad and I are going to go away on vacation in a week we're going to go away on a boat. We've arranged it so you can stay at Aunt Carol's you've always liked her."

He looked at both of us. We have talked about this, and we're expecting strong pushback from him, but he surprised us. "I think that would be nice. You're right. I like it at Aunt Carol's. She and I will eat ice cream every night."

Playfully I said, "Every night! Ice cream every night, god, maybe I should stay home with you and Carol."

Kay looked at me. "No, you're coming with me. We have issues to work out."

Joey added, "Sorry, Dad, you've got to go with Mom, but maybe they'll have ice cream on that boat you're going to be on. What's it like?"

Kay pulled up a chair, then went and got the brochures about the cruise, and sat down, and we started showing him where we were going to go. It felt like family.

He looked at both of us. "It looks nice; maybe someday the three of us could do something like this. But for now, I think it needs to be just you and Dad. But you got to bring me back a nice present."

Kay rubbed her hands through his hair. "I'm sure someday the three of us can do something like this. Any idea what you'd like for a present.?"

The two talked about what he may like for a present, he didn't want any T-shirts. I could feel a tear in the corner of my eye. I knew this whole ordeal had made him grow up and aged him, maybe a bit too quick, but I was also proud of his wisdom and how he seemed to understand what was going on. It was getting time for me to leave that night. It was so hard to leave. I wanted to stay and be a complete family. Kay looked at her watch, "Joey, I'm going to walk your father out to his car. I'll be back in a moment; please be ready for bed. We held hands walking to the car. We stared at the night sky together, then she kissed me, "It was a nice night, wasn't it? He seems to be doing pretty good despite all of it."

I pulled her closer. "A lot of that, no most of that has to do with you. You've done an excellent job with him while I've been missing in action." She squeezed my hand, letting me know she was excepting the compliment. We both knew it was time for me to go.

"Think about me tonight when you go to bed. The cruise is just a week away."

That next weekend we were on a flight to Miami where we would get on the ship. Kay was wearing a beautiful yellow sundress with blue flowers. It made her look like a sexy little farm girl going off to the big city. It was cut low to show off a lot of her cleavage. She leaned over in the flight sucked in her chest, giving me a good view down the dress. She always knew that I loved her breasts. "See anything you like, darling? Oh, by the way, I'm wearing the skimpiest of thongs underneath my dress. I don't even know if it covers my who-ha." Her pet name for her womanhood. I hadn't heard her use that word in years. She leaned in and whispered in my ear, "If this man weren't sitting next to me, I'd show you. Heck, maybe I will anyway, I don't think he'd mind, do you?" She was teasing me beyond belief like she had when we were dating. Kay had an incredible, delightful sexuality. It was one thing I loved about her, but it was also one of the first things to go as my alcoholism progressed. I couldn't blame her. Who would want a drunken lush slobbering and crawling all over them?

She then cuddled up to me and put her head on my shoulder. Kay wrapped her arm around mine and fell asleep. I gently woke her up as we were landing and said, "We're here, we're in Miami."

There was a bus at the airport collecting those of us going to be on the cruise. It was all so fun and exciting. I surprised myself by the fact I was enjoying it. It was a quick 15-minute ride over to the pier and another 20 minutes to get checked in. We were led to our cabin, and as soon as the door closed behind us, Kay was all over me, kissing me and grabbing at me while simultaneously taking her dress off. In seconds she was on the bed, her legs open, "Come on home, Bobby, time to come on home." For the next hour, we made crazy passionate love. We only to stop when we heard through the loudspeaker that all passengers had to grab their life vests and report to their staging areas. We quickly got dressed and made our way up to the staging area. We were probably looking like a disheveled mess talking pleasantries with other guests. As soon as the drill was over,

152

we were back in our room going crazy again. Around 7 o'clock that night, we both were hungry and got dressed. Our plan was to go to the buffet, eating as much as we could, and coming back and continuing our lovemaking.

The food tasted delicious, but I'm sure much of that was because of how starved we were, and the mood we were in our appetites were front and center stage. Kay had a couple of glasses of wine, something I was used to. She didn't have a drinking problem, I did. She was playing with my leg under the table with her foot letting me know that she was about full and wanted to get back to our suite. We were out to sea; by now, the sun had set. A beautiful moon drew us to the railing.

We stood there, arm in arm, saying little, then Kay spoke, "You know you're moving back into the house when the cruise is over."

"I figured that from want you said this afternoon, but it's nice to hear it come directly from your lips." She snuggled closer, and we just stood there in love again.

We then went back to our cabin. As we walked in, I notice that the bed had been turned down for the evening. And there on each pillow was a mint. The exact type of mint that had been at the crime scenes. Kay was in the middle of taking off her dress, and I yelled, "Oh my god, holy crap."

Kay just said, "What are you screaming about? I haven't even started yet."

I told her not to move. She was standing there, nude except for her panties trying to make sense of what was going on. The detective part of me kicked in. "Don't move, its evidence. It's like at the crime scene."

Kay responded, "A crime scene? I've done some strange things with you today, you might even say kinky, but I don't think we broken any laws, at least not yet."

153

Then I realized she had no idea what was going on or what I was ranting about. "Kay see the mints on our pillows those are the exact same type of mints that the killer we've been chasing has been leaving on the pillows of his victims."

Still, in a playful mood, she said, "Okay, arrest our cabin steward, but then let's get back to making love."

"Honey, please give me a few minutes you have no idea how big this is we're chasing a serial killer we've even nicknamed him, "The Mint Murderer."

"Kind of cute," she responded. When it came to police humor, she was as jaded as I was, having grown up in a cop family.

"Yeah, we didn't think it was that bad either. But Kay, this may be the breakthrough that we've been looking for. The mint is the clue he's been leaving us, taunting us with. For the first time, the message he has been leaving makes sense. I now know where he's been hunting, finding his victims on cruises like this one." She looked frustrated, wondering if we are going back to the old ways of work always taking precedence over her and our family. "Give me 10 minutes, please just 10 minutes."

"You've got five. I looked around and found the plastic bag that was to be used to hold ice in. Using a piece of paper, I gathered up the mints without touching them. Looking at them, I knew they were the same as we found at the different murder scenes. I put them in the little refrigerator made a quick couple of notes on a piece of paper. I was going to have to call Alex and the captain tomorrow. I wanted to let them know what I was thinking. "Okay, honey, where were we." She smiled, glad that I had kept my promise about letting her come before the job.

"Remember that thing I talked about showing you a couple of weeks ago---well. Kay laid down on the bed, holding a vibrator up and smiled, "Meet my friend for the last three years we're going to put on a show for you."

We didn't leave the room until 10:30 the next morning, I was letting her and her needs come before work. "You know, sweetie. I need to call back and talk to Alex and Colleen this is big, really big."

"I get it, and thanks! In the past, you would've been calling them last night and talking all night instead of doing what we were doing all night. "Take as much time as you want, you're a good detective, and I know how important what you're working on is, there are families out there wanting answers. I'll be out near the pool I'll be the one wearing the skimpiest bikini and get something to eat you're going to need your strength you've got many years of sexual back taxes to pay."

I called the station, luckily. Alex was there. "Alex, something's come up is the captain there?"

"Yes, what the hell is going on?"

"Is Sandy there?"

"Yes, But, once again, what the hell is going on."

"I've got something important to tell all three of you, so get in the conference room and call me back at this number."

"What the hell is it? Kay can't be pregnant already." Just for a second, I thought about the vasectomy Kay had me get during the middle of my drinking, not wanting to have any more children with me.

"No, it's about the case. It's really important."

About five minutes later, the phone rang. "Are you all there?"

"Yes, we're all here now. What the hell is going on?

"The mint. Last night when Kay and I walked into our suite, the bed was turned down and what was on our pillows but mints -- the exact same

155

type of mints we been finding that the crime scene. I think he's been hunting and finding his victims on cruises." There was a quietness then

Capt. Colleen spoke up, "My god, that makes sense. We thought it was hotels, but maybe it's cruises. Nice work. This is really big! Why didn't you call us last night?"

"Excuse me, Captain, I don't mean to be rude or disrespectful to you or your rank but go fuck yourself." They all laughed, including Capt. Colleen.

Capt. said, "It's nice to see that you got your priorities back in line."

"I saved the mints. When I get done here, I'll take a picture so you can see the brand and how they're the same ones from the crime scenes. I'll send the pictures to Susan, and she can start doing her magic."

Alex spoke up. "Partner, I don't want to hear any more from you until you're back in the office. We'll probably have a lot to go over them. But you get back to Kay and enjoy yourselves. By the way, what does her new bikini look like? I hear through the grapevine that she was doing some serious shopping?"

"Oh, enjoy myself that I will. I've got to go find her now. She said she'd be up by the pool." I was enjoying teasing Alex. "She told me she'd be the one in the skimpiest bikini. I saw it when she took it out of the suitcase, I've seen postage stamps there're bigger than it. I'm very much looking forward to getting back to her. I bet you want pictures, buddy, but I'm not going to take any."

The Cap. chimed in, "Okay, Okay, we're going to go now. The three of us will try and start figuring out what this mint thing means and see where it takes us. Bobby, I don't want to hear anything more from you until I see you walking through the door of the precinct next Monday. And stop talking about Kay and her skimpy postage stamp size bikini. Those are images I don't want in my head, and I surely don't want them in Alex's; he'll never get anything done. Enjoy yourselves, and Bobby, thanks, thanks for the good detective work. But mostly, thanks for what you're doing for your family."

We hung up. I went to the room, got out the two mints took some pictures of them, and hit send knowing they soon be in Susan's care. I then went to the 24-hour buffet and loaded up. I knew I would need my strength. Kay was back to being her crazy sexual self. One reason I fell in love with her. I didn't know when I might get a chance to eat again. I was going crazy scarfing down food when Kay came up to me. She had her cover-up on, but it didn't cover up much. The bikini was as small as I thought it was, postage stamps. She put something down on the table, "Take this! You'll need it."

I asked her what it was. "It's Viagra, the only drug I ever want you taking ever again. Don't worry, the doctor gave me a prescription, and I've got a large jar of it back in the room."

"I'm not that old plus you know I don't have that much trouble getting an erection."

"It's not about getting an erection. It's about longevity. It's about keeping it hard for a long, long time. You know what they say in the ads if your erection lasts more than four hours, call a doctor, that's what we're going for if yours last more than four hours we're going to the ship's chapel and light a candle of thanks. Maybe you should take two? What was it you would say during your drinking if one were good two was always better."

"Let's start with one." I took the pill as she went up to the buffet. She was scaring me.

She came back and asked me how the phone call went.

"Excellent, very well, everybody agrees this is the best led we've had yet in this damn case at least we know where he's hunting that makes a lot less ground for us to cover."

157

We had a nice casual lunch, but then she smiled looked at her watch, "it's been about 45 minutes let's go see how that pill works. She grabbed my hand. "Come on, I've got something back in our cabin I want to show you—me! I've got to get out of this bikini I feel so--well covered up."

As we walked along, the old Kay kept talking, "Honey, you wouldn't believe some of the things I've learned about pleasuring oneself during these years we've been apart. I've got so much to teach you, so much to show you, so many things I want you to do to me." She was again starting to scare me, really scare me. Thank God recovery had taught me to surrender and go with the flow, I knew I was on a new and different river one I had never been on before and Kay was the captain; my job was just to row the boat.

Chapter 24

◆

We were out to sea when the news was disseminated to the crew and passengers. It was printed in the daily news tablet that the ship put out each day.

"We regret to announce that one of our crewmembers, a Riche Teem, was found murdered in Tokyo. He was the victim of an apparent robbery gone bad. He had been with the company for two short years. He leaves back in Iran, a mother and father, and two younger sisters. There will be a wreath in the ship's chapel if you'd like to stop by and say a prayer for him and his family. Tomorrow evening at sunset, we will be giving the wreath to the ocean as our way to honor Riche's memory. The small service will be on the back of the boat if you'd like to join the crew in saying goodbye to one of their own."

They were working on getting ahead of the narrative, knowing that the news would come out. The captain and the company were doing an excellent job of it. Angela's appearance was scarce that next day.

I watched the brief service from my balcony. I notice it Angela was not there, and there were few women at the ceremony, his reputation must've gotten out. Magdalene was there. As a captain threw the wreath into the ocean, I raised my glass of scotch, "Made the worms find some use for you. You had none here."

I spent the evening in my cabin, in case for some reason I have been discovered which I didn't believe to be true, this had been an easy kill. There is a plastic one shotgun that would pass through any metal detector underneath the pillow, not more than two feet from me just in case. It would be more for use on me than on anyone else I had sworn to myself I would never be taken. It was a quiet evening as I thought it would be. I had food delivered around 10 o'clock and then went to bed sleeping like a baby.

The next morning when I woke up, standing there at the end of my bed, looking studying me was Angela. My hand moved, moved to the gun underneath the pillow. After a bit, when she saw I was awake, she came and sat on the bed next to me. She was holding a copy of the ship's newspaper with the announcement. She stared at me, looking for something trying to put things together in her mind. "You did this, didn't you? I know you did! Why?" There was no judgment in her voice, just curiosity.

"He hurt you. He made you feel that you weren't special; besides, it's what I do." In these past ten seconds, she now knew more about me than anyone else ever had.

"You killed him for me? You killed him because he had hurt me? Because he had touched my womanhood when I didn't want him to?

My confession continued, "Yes, it's called justice. For you but other women too. I'm sure this Riche has done worst to other women." I knew my life would be different from that moment on, but I had no idea how or how long my life might be lasting. If she turned me in, things would be over quickly.

She added, "No one has ever protected me before. No one is ever killed for me before. Did you know I wanted him dead?

"No, I didn't know that. I just wanted you to feel safe. Death creates a certain type of safety."

Grabbing Daniel's hand and gently holding it, Angela shared, "I had wanted to hurt him bad, real, bad, many times in my head. I have thought about ways to hurt him and do what you did to him. Did he suffer, I hope?"

160

"No, there wasn't time he died within seconds, but you're safe, and he has paid for what he did, those were my goals. You don't have to worry about him anymore. That's all that matters."

"Daniel, what you didn't know or maybe you do was that he had been successful with another girl on the ship. He successfully took from a young 20-year-old girl from India what wasn't his to take. She was engaged to be married. She was working on the ship to get money for her wedding. Her fiancé works on another ship for both her and her man are poor. She was a virgin. He took her maidenhood. She's now worries her fiancé will not want to marry her now, she's not pure anymore."

"I didn't know that. I even feel better about what I did. But I did it to protect only you. Riche would've tried with you again, and if he were successful, he would've hurt you bad. What you did to him was bruise his pride when you got away from him. Men like Riche can't stand to have their ego's bruised. He would've tried again towards the end of the voyage, not caring if he lost his job. He would've gotten most of his wages by then, and he would have his revenge for you hurting his pride. Angela, you can't tell anyone what you know, not even the girl he raped! No one!"

Softly and gently with much compassion, she looked me directly in the eyes there was a peace and quiet within them, "Daniel, I know that, I understand that, don't worry your secret is my secret. This isn't the first time for you, is it?" She now had that curious questioning look on her face again, staring at me, she was searching me for something more than just answers. She was trying to see and make sense of what was happening between us and inside of her. She wanted to know who I was and for some strange reason, I wanted to tell her.

"No, it's not. I'm a thief, and in the process of being a thief, I've killed many people." Now she knew everything about me, well not everything but enough to start putting things together.

"You must be good."

"I am very good."

"Now that I know, are you going to kill me?" She asked, I think, already knowing the answer.

I stared into her eyes and said something I had never said before, "No, of course not! I could never hurt you; I love you." My words scared me for they were real, and I had never loved anyone before. She stared at me, looking to see if I was sincere telling the truth. She was good at reading people.

"You've never been in love before, have you?"

"No"

She looked at me, "Me neither. But I know I love you too. I have from the first day I saw you on that other voyage." What she said scared both of us, "Well, I've got to go. I've got things I need to do. Things need to look normal. You need to be around the ship as if nothing has happened. We will talk later. And Daniel, know that your secrets are safe with me." Things were reversed. She was now working to protect me. She then came and kissed me. I pulled her to me and kissed her back. My world was now as different as it was after my first kill.

For the first time in my life, I felt powerless. I have put my life in another's hands. Being under someone else's control had never gone well before. But this was the first time I did it by choice. I wanted to believe it would be different this time, but I didn't know. Angela left, I got up showered, got dressed, and went down to have breakfast. My paper was waiting for me as were the eggs benedict I had ordered the day before. I sat there a bit longer than usual, eating slowly reading the newspaper but taking nothing in. My mind was back to Angela sitting on my bed this morning I kept reliving it and what I had said and felt but mainly what she had said.

I talked with the passengers at the table next to me. I had seen them attending the funeral preformed, by the captain. We did the typical small

162

talk about how unpredictable life is and how one needs to live to its fullest within the moment. It was a friendly and pleasant conversation. That night at the poker table, Riche's death was the main subject of talk. I listened more, then I talked. Eugene was making his standard remarks about how if he had been home because of the gun he always carried on him, the situation would have gone different had it been him. "Where do you keep it?"

He patted his side, "I'm a lefty, but I'm quick."

"And your other one?" He looks surprised that I knew about it. I just shrugged my shoulders.

Eugene smiled, "Smart! Around my ankle." Paul then pulled the conversation in a different direction.

I was wondering when I would see Angela again as I walked back to my suite. As I stood outside my door, getting out my card to open it, I could smell the fragrance of orchids. It was subtle and sweet. I figured somebody had walked by shortly before me wearing the scent. I liked it.

I walked in the door, and the smell was stronger. I looked over, and lying in bed with the sheets pulled up to her neck was Angela. Her beautiful black hair framed her face. She had a black choker with one rhinestone in the middle around her neck. I stared at her, then walked over to where she was and undressed. When I was nude, I slid under the covers, and she snuggled up to me in her nakedness. She wrapped her thigh over my leg, took her arm, and draped it over my chest, her head resting on my shoulder. I could feel her small breasts and nipples pressing up against me, her head resting on my shoulder.

I said something, and she took her finger and held it to my lips. "No words tonight, Daniel, no words tonight." She was right. I could feel they would have gotten in the way. We laid like that for hours until we fell asleep in each other's arms. In the morning, when we woke up, we made love each of us working to give in to the other. I had only had sex before that morning; for the first time, I was making love being in love. We then got up and showered. Angela put on the fresh uniform she had brought with her. We kissed, and she went on her way, telling me she would see me that afternoon like always. I dressed and went to have breakfast, more content and happier than I ever had been before in my life. Someone knew me for who I was, a stone-cold killer, and still wanted me and wasn't afraid of me. I spent most of the day walking around the ship thinking and contemplating wondering what the future would be like. I had loved that when I got into bed, all she was wearing was that black choker with a rhinestone in the middle of it. She had laid it out on my dresser with a little note, "Think of me."

I took the choker to the ship's jewelry store, for I knew they had a jewelry smith who worked there. I asked him if he could replace the rhinestone with a diamond of about the same size. He told me that would not be a problem at all. We agreed on a price and a diamond. He reassured me that would be done before supper that night. That afternoon Angela came to my suite at the same time she always did. We talked about what was happening on the ship and what was being said about Riche's death. There were not any red lights or alarms going off from what she could tell. As we talked, we held hands even though hers were callused from a life of hard work to me; her skin was the softest I had ever felt. She kept telling me and giving me information about Yangs and the Dohms.

She turned to me. "Are you going to rob one of them?"

"Probably both!"

"Are you going to kill them?"

Knowing there could be no lies between us, nothing except complete honesty, I answered, "Yes."

"And the Tiedens?"

"No, he keeps very little money and jewelry at home."

"Makes sense." I could see Angela's mind working, putting it all together. She was relaxed as we talked, she continued holding my hand

164

never flinching at the information she got just rubbing her thumb back and forth on my skin.

"It's none of my business what are you worth--- a lot?"

"Millions."

"Why haven't you stopped?" It was a good question, one I never had the answer to until now.

"I've never had a reason to stop. Not until today. Will you marry me?"

She squeezed my hand, "Probably Daniel, but right now I can't, you're a murderer I'm still trying to wrap my head around that. I'm in love with a murderer. But I will be with you for as long as you want the rest of our lives hopefully then maybe someday, maybe someday soon I will marry you. I've got so many questions."

"Can you stop?"

"I can, but I have to finish with these two, then I know we will be set for life."

"What is your plan for after when you're done." It was a good question.

"Angela, that part is not that developed. At worst, I would die doing what I do best, or I saw myself slipping away, getting lost in some country vanishing becoming a ghost."

"If you really plan on stopping, that makes a difference. Can I help you with this? Would it be okay if I think about this?" I told her absolutely that part of what I loved about her was how smart and intelligent she was. She smiled.

"You know if you didn't have a conscience, you'd be good at what I do." She smiled again.

165

"Who knows, but I do know I want you to teach me to be a warrior. You are a warrior with a purpose not always a good purpose but a purpose. "Will you teach me to be a warrior, I hated the feeling of not been able to fight him off."

"But you did."

"No, I was lucky, I was lucky that object was there or else it would've been a different outcome."

"Warriors do train and develop their skills, but they also use what's around them like you did. But yes, I'll teach you how to fight and defend yourself."

She said she had to go. We kissed and off she went into that other world. I knew she would be there waiting for me after the poker game. It went well that night I made $15,000 at the table enough to pay for the diamond that the jeweler had placed on Angela's choker.

When I got back from the game, she was under the sheets waiting but with a nervous look on her face. "Have you seen my choker? I wanted to be wearing it when you got back?"

I reached inside my pocket and pulled it out, dangling it in the air, "You mean this one? I had the jeweler make an alteration." Her eyes were wide open; I went over to the bed, showed it to her, and put it around her neck.

"Oh my god, is that a..."

"Diamond, yes, yes, it is. No more rhinestones for you. Do you like it?" She answered me by climbing on top of me. Touching me until I was ready to be inside of her, all the time staring me in the eyes until the moments her ecstasy automatically closed them. She drifted off into bliss, slowly rocking back and forth on me. We fell asleep that night in each other's arms again; we both wanted to stay connected to each other.

Again, in the morning, we made love and showered and got ready to start our days each in different worlds.

"I want to leave it in your suite! It wouldn't be safe in my cabin. Can you put it in your safe for me?"

"14-17-51," she looked at me.

"It's the combination to the safe just put it in there yourself. I'm assuming you'll be wanting to be wearing it again tonight when I get back from the poker game."

Angela went over twirled the combination, the door open, and she saw the stacks of bills in there. She looked at me, "You trust me with knowing the combination." I laughed; she sounded so naïve.

"My love, you know more about me than anybody ever has and yes, could destroy me in a moment if you wanted. But I truly believe you love me too," then I change my tone to one of joking, "and besides, we're on a ship in the middle of the ocean where are you going to go? I meant it; I want to be with you forever." She put the choker in the safe, smiled, and closed the door. Kissed me and left.

Chapter 25

◆

The cruise ship landed back in Miami on the morning of the next Saturday. We caught a shuttle to the airport, and by 10:30, we were on our plane heading back to Phoenix. The cruise had been successful in its purpose, a complete reconnection between Kay and myself. Sexually she had totally worn me out. I'd forgotten what a wanton and lustful woman I had married. She had put all those feelings away during the last few years of my addiction and these early years of recovery. But now that she trusted I would be staying sober, "Turning my life over to care," she was letting it out in some pretty scary ways. I kidded her telling her I thought she had a strange sexual addiction. I had learned active addiction shortens a person's life by 15 years. I teased her that I thought her sexual appetite would shorten my life by 15 years. She would just smile. "Maybe so, Bobby, maybe so, but when you've squeezed the toothpaste out of the tube, you can't put it back. And you'll die with a smile on your face."

That's Saturday afternoon, we went to the apartment where I had been living these past years. Kay and never been to it. We put all my recovery books in a box, placing my Alcoholics Anonymous "Big Book" on top. Inside, it had been signed by all the people in my unit, the Tiebout unit, named after Dr. Harry Tiebout, one of the early researchers in why Alcoholics Anonymous worked for some and not for others. All the people who had helped save my life had signed the book; there was Bill H., Anthony F., Andrew I., Fernando Q., George K., Leo E., Daniel L., Matthew Y. Jerry F., Randolph T., and Jim S., our counselor. Underneath each of their names was their sobriety date, and a little message each had inscribed. Things like, "Never look back except to do your inventory," "Live and Let Live," "May your life be like a camel traveling to the best of times and the worst of times but knowing how to stay dry." Each one of them meaning the world to me, especially Fernando Q. who had been my roommate. He had written, "Thank you for the struggles, and your honesty may your life be as rich and real as ours was here together." We always kidded that between the 10 of us, there was probably one complete person. Under Jim's guidance, we were using it to complete each other. The book would be next to my bed at home.

We packed up my clothes that I would keep it all fit into two suitcases. There were three boxes of other odds and ends mainly cooking utensils we could use at home everything fit in the backseat and trunk of my car. As we're walking down the sidewalk to my car Kay took the "Big Book" it was on top of the box of books I was carrying brought it to her chest, clinging to it and said, "Honey, let's go home."

I looked back, and she said, "Doesn't one of your inscriptions say never look back except to do your inventory." I nudged her, "Yeah." We waited around another five minutes until the Salvation Army truck rolled up. I gave them the keys, "It's unit seven. Everything in there is for the Army." I had made a deal with them; they could have everything in there if they would clean it up sufficient enough that I could get my damage deposit back. "When you've got it cleaned up, leave the keys on the counter, the landlord will be stopping by later to check out the apartment and to pick up the keys.

It felt strange walking back into the house, knowing that I wouldn't be leaving again. We started putting things away, then Kay told me to stick out my hand, and inside it, she placed one of her little blue pills. "Joey won't be home until tomorrow night. We've got reinitiate our bed and the other rooms in the house. I've ordered takeout, and by the time we finish putting your stuff away and eating, it'll be about 45 minutes." She had been quite impressed by how well the Viagra had worked on the ship.

Sunday night, Aunt Carol brought Joe home. He ran up the driveway and hugged us both. "You're back home; Dad, aren't you? Aunt Carol explained everything to me."

Carol, who had been pretty frosty to me during my drinking years and recovery, walked up to me gave me a big hug and kiss on the cheek, "Welcome home, Bobby, welcome home, we start anew."

Joey looked at me. "Dad, your crying, why? Isn't your coming home a good thing."

I got down on my knees in front of him, held him, and looked him square in the eyes, "Joey, this is the best thing ever. What I learned in treatment is there are different types of tears. Still, almost all of it has to do with meaning. When meaningful things get taken away, there are tears, but when meaningful things are returned, there are even more tears I'm so grateful for being returned to you and mom. That's what my tears are about, you two mean so much to me.

He looked at Kay and her tears. "And you, Mom?"

"The same thing, sweetie."

"And yours, Aunt Carol."

"Ditto."

Kay saved us. "Okay, gang enough of this closeness I got some ribs in the oven that are ready to go on the grill. Joey, you and your dad are in charge of grilling, Carol and me we'll get everything else we need from the kitchen for a good old family barbecue." Half an hour later, we were all sitting around the picnic table, laughing and celebrating my homecoming. Kay brought out a present of a large sand dollar and a giant starfish for our son. He loved his gifts. Kay had picked them up at the ship's boutique when I was attending a "Friends of Bill W's" meeting held every day on the ship. I never missed one. They were enjoyable meetings, plus they gave me a welcome break from Kay's appetites teetering on perversions. We finish the meal with Kay bringing out a Dairy Queen frozen cake. Joey's favorite written on the top in frosting was, "Welcome home, Dad." Aunt Carol took a picture of the three of us with me holding it. I decided I was going to put it on my desk at work.

That Monday, I was back to work after a nice breakfast with Kay and Joey. I walked into the conference room. Written above, each couple was the date/s of the cruise or cruises they had taken. Captain Colleen walked into the room and gave me a big hug, "Bobby, you wouldn't believe how busy it's been around here. That lead you gave us hasn't solved it, but it's giving us a hell of a lot to work on. We all agree his hunting ground has been cruise ships. We're clos,e very close."

I asked, "You must've crossed referenced names on each of the cruisers."

"Well, there is where we have a problem."

"What is he changing identities with each cruise? And with the money he's been making from the robberies, he could easily afford it. You can get a good quality passable passport for $1000. For a bit more, well, you can get quality, top quality I suspected he's in this category," She was just listening. "What about photos. I know on this cruise we took our pictures were taken when we entered." That's a relatively new thing most of the old ones they just went with passports."

Captain Colleen spoke up. "No, we think his identity is the same but…" and then she paused for a bit it was clear there was a hitch. "We are working on getting all the warrants and paperwork we need to get the information from all the different cruise lines. They're stalling us. It would be a complete nightmare for them publicity-wise if it got out that someone was stalking passengers on cruise lines robbing and murdering them. Somehow when we get all the data, this will be easily solvable, but that's going to take some work politics are now involved. Bobby everything stalled out. It's been that way for a couple of days now." I stared at the whiteboards, but I was furious inside.

Just about then, Sandy and Alex walked in. I got big hugs from both of them, even Alex, who's not a hugger. "Damn buddy, everything's changed since we know where he's hunting. Every one of these folks had been on a cruise or multiple cruises within the year before their murders.

171

It's strange, but some people cruise a hell of a lot. We got one couple that had been on eight cruises in the year before they were murdered. In fact, we've only got one that had been on one cruise in the past year. How about you and Kay; are you signed up to go on another?"

"Well, I think our case is a little different it was kind of a honeymoon. A get reacquainted type of thing, but I would go again it was very nice having people there to take care of your every need. They really pampered us pretty good, and the food was delicious, and always was; I mean always was available."

"Nice, but what about this bikini Kay was wearing? Was it really as small as a postage..." Sandy interrupted Alex, "back to the case, let him have his memories. Welcome home, welcome back to our shit storm. You wouldn't believe how political and uncomfortable this has become. They're treating us like we're going after their livelihood instead of trying to help them catch people who been killing their passengers."

In treatment, Bobby had learned about empathy stepping into somebody else's shoes. "I know I've just gotten back and haven't been around the last few days, but how many different cruise lines are we dealing with?"

Sandy said, "Eight."

"Well, I would be protective too. If this got out, the cruise lines would be besieged with cancellations, and their stocks would plummet. We can't let them think we're the enemy or treat them like they are our enemy. It's just going to take some time. It's not like he hasn't been around for a long time."

Alex added, "But he's probably out there hunting right now, or maybe he's stepping off a cruise following his next victim, I want to get him before the son of a bitch kills again. I think that should be our goal."

"You're right, partner. We all want that, but it's going to take some time, but we're almost there."

172

Captain Colleen spoke up, "But because of the politics Chief of Police Stan Maysack is now involved, so the pace has slowed down a bit." With just the mention of his name, all four of us gave the finger to the heavens.

I looked over at the other board, the one that had pictures of our budding psychopaths, "Any new news on the three of them?"

"Nothing, it's like to three of them never existed after their childhood."

"They must be the cream of the crop."

The rest of the day was spent with me going over the files. I was getting up to date on all the information. The three of them had put together since my phone call. Plus, reading lots of correspondence between the cruise lines lawyers, our department, Chief of Police Stan Maysack, and the city's lawyers. There was talk about getting the FBI involved, but we wanted to keep the case ours, four of the people had been killed in our state, two in our city. We found him. We wanted to be the ones to close it out, and we all knew Jim Syverson's warning strong suggestion, to take him down like the mad dog he was. The FBI would want to capture him, test him, and study him. They were into those things. But we had in front of us a board with pictures of all those he had killed. It was now personal.

At the end of the day, before we were to go home, I asked the three into the conference room. "I got a little something for each of you for the way you picked up the load so that Kay and I could go on this, well I'll call it a second honeymoon. Maybe I should say it was our first honeymoon Kay reminded me that I got pretty drunk and stayed drunk most of the time on our first one.

"They're all the same. Please open the boxes I'm excited to see what you think." They all ripped into the wrappings, then they looked at what I had gotten them they looked at me, and all of them together said, "Fuck you!" I have bought each a box of mints, the same type that the killer had used. They were selling them in the gift store on the ship. "Cop humor guys, cop humor." Captain Colleen gave me the finger. Alex was unwrapping one and putting it in his mouth. "Mummmm, they're actually delicious. I'm glad I didn't know that, or I would've eaten the evidence I love good chocolate. Then Sandy and Colleen had to try one. They left them in the conference room for us to snack on when going over the case.

Chapter 26

◆

For the first time in my life, I had something that I didn't want to lose or ever give up. The thought of total retirement was growing on me. I have pretty much decided to take out both the Yangs and the Dohms. Not in some ritualistic way like I had in the past. But this time in a simple rob and kill. There would be no tucking them in bed, so they laid there peacefully like my parents. The one good memory I had from my childhood. There would be no mints. Once. I had the combinations and Randell's eye being recognized by the safe, they would be dead. None of these murder robberies would look like the others to the detectives chasing me. It would have been as if I disappeared after the murders of Gill and Mary Deutsch. It was the first time in my life I didn't want the police chasing me. No challenges would be offered.

We probably had enough now if I cashed everything in. Still, I knew in the quick departure that we would be taking, percentage would be lost to those I would be selling the gold and silver to in exchange for untraceable high-end diamonds. The currency of a thieve on the move.

Also, much of my cash would be needed to be turned into euros. I needed extremely high-end passports for both Angela and myself---two sets. One set would indicate that we were from Canada, but our backup passports would have us formerly living in France. A language Angela spoke fluently. From everything they were saying, I conservatively estimated that I would get 2 million from the Yangs and the Dohms. That should cover the cost of the exchanges allowing me to keep the 7 or 8 million I presently had. All of this, I was talking over with Angela. I wanted her to know everything and that I was serious about giving up my lifestyle to be with her. The cruise was close to being over.

"We're going to need a place to go, too, a place to go get lost in. Big cities were best for that we decided to go to Ho Chi Minh City it would be a good place to start. Now that the Vietnam war was over and had been for decades, there were enough foreigners that we wouldn't stand out, plus Angela's French was near perfect. Angela eventually wanted to live over in the area near Laos. An area where the Huong had come from and still lived. She had been there once and fell in love with its lush green rolling mountains. It also came out that she spoke Hmong and enough Vietnamese that we could get by. I was finding out so much about her. "How many languages do you know? "Four well and three more where I could get by. Eight if you count Canadian---Aaa."

"Daniel, the ship docks for two days in Ho Chi Minh City. I can get the time off we can easily fly to the area I want you to see; you can see for yourself the beautiful hills, mountains, and valleys where I want us to live someday. Maybe you'll love it too."

"I'd love to go there."

"I would need some money for flights. Would you be willing to give me some?"

"Sweetie, (which was now what I was always calling her when we were alone), you know the combination to the safe, take what you need." She sat down on the desk using the computer, made some calculations went to the safe, took out precisely what you thought we would need. Before she closed the door, I told her to take a little more, telling her that unexpected things can always come up.

"We have to be careful our monies will have to last our lifetime. You won't be doing what you do anymore." I laughed. She was frugal, not just beautiful. But what I loved, even more, she was talking about us as a couple, as a lifetime couple.

At night while we laid in bed, we would take out the computer, look over and study Ho Chi Minh City. Angela was looking for places to live,

176

things to do and see. I was looking for areas of safety and routes of escape if needed. The evening would always end with us looking for and looking at pictures of the hills and valleys up in Phongsaly Province in Laos, where Angela wanted us to settle eventually. She had a particular and unique spot on the slopes of Mount Phu Fa near where she had a stay one night years ago.

I told her I thought we would probably live in Ho Chi Minh City for a period of time" before moving to the hills. "We need to make sure we're good and lost, and no one's chasing us before we move out of the city. There are always more places to hide in a city. Plus, there would be things I would need that were still easier to get within an anonymous city than in the countryside. I would not be risking carrying guns with me when I flew to Vietnam. I would need to get some of these tools in Vietnam. My job would still be to protect Angela.

Evening poker games were going well. I was gaining substantial information that would make the robberies easier and winning a few bucks in the process. Like Peter in the past had been my true poker competition, it was now Paul. He was an outstanding poker player; the rest were mediocre at best. I looked forward to taking out Randall. His egotistical narcissistic attitude plus the fact that he was fat and ugly but saw himself as a lady's man sickened me. But he would've never known it. There would be some regrets with Eugene for the more I got to know him, the more he and his wife seemed like Gil and Mary, a lovely couple truly in love. I listened to him, seeking advice on how to be a good husband. I already saw Angela and me as married. He would give me good advice. Randall would always want to throw in his repugnant opinion. Always be sure and give it to her hard, and deep women like it rough that the only way to keep them truly happy. I thought to myself. "I'll be giving it to you rough" you jerk. Everybody at the table took his comments as bullshit except for him. He surely knew how to make money, but he had no idea how to be a husband. Just observing him and Ivana together for five minutes made that obvious.

The day we docked in Ho Chi Minh City was a light rainy day. Angela was so excited to be taking me to the slopes of Mount Phu Fa. I wanted to spend as much time there as possible. So, when we got to the airport, I took out the extra money I had brought along hired a private pilot. He could fly us there; we could get there four hours before the other flight would've arrived. At no extra charge, he would hang around and fly back the next day for the weather conditions looked good. Angela had booked us a night at the only resort in the area high in the hills overlooking her favorite valley. We hired a driver for just dollars a day who would be with us and at our call until we left. After we checked in at the resort, Angela wanted to show me her most favorite spot in the whole world. We left the driver at the resort and hiked out, going further up into the hills. Angela was so excited to see if it was still the way she remembered it.

We turned a corner, and there was a plateau area, and off to the right was a small waterfall and a stream. Angela grabbed my hand and took me to the edge of the stream, where it became another waterfall falling about 100 feet. "Look see down in the village that's small stream it's the same one we are standing next to right now. When I was here last, I hiked up following the stream, and I found this place I call it heaven, I know it's hokey, but if there is a heaven, this is what it would look like." We stood there staring down into the valley. You could see three other waterfalls on the surrounding hillsides that we surmise likely came together somewhere down there in the valley.

"Will explore them all when we live here." I told her, "and we'll build our home right here, right here on this plateau."

She just smiled, "I hope you love it as much as I do."

"I do, sweetie, I do."

Angela reached into her backpack, took out a blanket, and laid it on the ground. She then stood up and took off all her clothes. Standing there nude with the hills as a backdrop, she smiled. "My sweet Daniel, make love to me here. Make love to me here in Heaven." About three hours later, we were back hiking down the trail heading to the resort. We had a beautiful meal of traditional food made right in front of us on the veranda. We invited our driver to eat with us, but he refused, saying he'd already eaten, which we knew wasn't true. We retired to our room built on one of the outcroppings overlooking the valley. We sat on the balcony until the stars came out.

Light rain clouds were moving in, so we retired to the bedroom, pulled the mosquito netting around the bed, got undressed, and just laid there staring out at the stars until the clouds and rain came. As the rain gently made music on the roof, Angela turned to me. "I'll marry you. But you need to know I can't have children, that my secret. If you still want me, we can have the captain marry us in your suite on the ship. We can be married by Monday."

"Don't you want a big ceremony and your mother and grandmother there? And by the way, I don't want children; I just want you as my wife. I don't want to share you with anyone."

"Good, I want to be married to you. I want to be Mrs. Daniel Ray."

"Well, about that,, Daniel Ray isn't my real name; it's one of mine many aliases."

I told her my real name. "Stop Daniel! To me, you'll always be Daniel Ray, and I'll be Mrs. Daniel Ray."

"Okay, but when we travel back here, we will have different passports with different names. How about I let you pick out our new names, just make them sound Canadian."

She scrunched up her face. "What do Canadian names sound like?"

"I have no idea that will be yours to solve but probably something with heritages dating back to France or England. Maybe go with something French that will suit you better, but don't make me sound Frenchie." She loved the idea and immediately thought of new names for each.

"Can I go see my mother and grandmother and say a final goodbye to them?"

"Absolutely, in fact, it would be best if we took different routes getting back here. But we'll need to meet once in Oregon. Eventually, we'll meet in Ho Chi Minh City at a specific hotel. I'll get here a couple of days before to get and set up an apartment."

"Don't you want my help with that."

"No, during this first year will be about making sure that we're not being hunted, I would like to pick the places we live in the city. All will need to have a good clean escape route. You get to lay out what our home in Heaven will be like."

We laid out details I told her how I would be getting our monies changed over into diamonds easily transportable. We would also have a certain amount of cash. I will be mailing bundles of currency to different hotels around the city where I would have rooms booked.

"You'll know that you're going to have to be carrying some diamonds and your beautiful vagina. Also, up in your backside just as I will."

The thought of it made her laugh, "You mean I really will have a million-dollar muff."

I answered, "And your ass will be worth a lot more than that you can always get more up there." The only problem is when you have to go to the bathroom, do it in a way where you don't flush the diamonds down into the sewer. But they will be in special packets to protect against that and will go over all that."

She just laughed, "You are bringing me into your world, aren't you? Do you want me to kill someone?"

"No, sweetie, I just want you to pack your sweetness full of diamonds." We eventually fell asleep.

180

I woke in the morning. Angela was gently kissing my chest when she saw I was awake. She crawled up to kiss me. "Good morning, fiancé, good morning." She continued passionately kissing and touching me until I was ready. She then crawled on top. She wanted to make love to me. I laid there looking up at her beautiful face. Her eyes were closed. She was biting her lip in ecstasy. Her jet-black hair hung across her chest, covering her breasts as she rocked back and forth on me. She would bring me to the brink and then stop. Looking down, smiling at me, then she would start again. She did this several times when Angela was ready; she grabbed me tight. I grabbed her, and we finished together. We then had an excellent breakfast overlooking Angela's Heaven. I spend some time talking to the resort owner working on who owned the land Heaven would be built on. He was sure it was a local farmer. The family owned most of the hill. They had brought their parcel of land from him.

After breakfast, Angela was packing things up, getting ready for us to go back to the ship. I stood on the ledge, staring down into the valley, watching the birds as they soared back-and-forth, riding the thermals looking for prey. Angela was right; this would be a little piece of Heaven, but before we would be back here, I had to do the work of hell. I said to myself, "But wasn't Lucifer, nothing but a fallen Angel."

Our driver, always a quiet older man, took us back to the outskirts of the airport where the pilot was waiting for us. Once we got back to Ho Chi Minh City, we caught a cab and made our way back to the ship, but on the way, I saw beautiful pearl laden white dress in a store window we stopped and got it. It would be Angela's wedding dress. I ran down the street to a jewelry store I had seen and bought two simple gold bands not knowing her size I had the woman try it on she saw my questioning look, "It can always be re-sized." I bought the two gold bands and a pearl necklace which would look perfect with her wedding dress because of its cut.

When we got back to the ship, I talked to the captain, telling him about Angela and me, which he already knew about. "I want to marry Angela, and she wants to marry me, and because we met on the ship, we'd

181

like to be married on the ship. We will have a larger ceremony later. I would like you to marry us in our suite tomorrow—a private discrete ceremony her, me, and you."

"You'll need two witnesses. I can bring along the first mate, and I'm sure Angela has a good friend who will witness for her and can be discreet. I will give you all the papers you will be officially married, but you need to get them certified back in the states. Congratulations, I've known her for some years. She's a perfect woman and quite beautiful." I could hear a touch of envy in the captain's voice; I think he had a crush on her. "After you're married, she can stay with you like she already has been doing, but it will be legal. We'll keep her cabin the way it is for discretion."

The next day in a simple ceremony in my suite, we were married. I gave her a simple gold wedding band with the date and the word "forever" engraved inside it. To my surprise, her ring fit perfectly. She gave me my ring. We wore them on different fingers until the end of the voyage.

Two days later, the voyage would end in Singapore. The last night's goodbyes were said to poker buddies over a scotch and a Havana. Everyone would be flying to their different homes. From there, I had all the information I needed on the Yangs and the Dohms. I told the captain I had found what I wanted on the cruise, and we wanted to get home and start our new life together, and I wanted my family to meet Angela. In truth, I had no family; she was my family. We joked we had already had our honeymoon just before the wedding.

The first thing I did as I stepped off the ship took the ring and put it on the correct finger. Angela had already done that. "I so much want to be Mrs. Daniel Ray, or whatever your name. I put my ring on the correct finger, this morning, and I couldn't take it off."

There was so much to do; we immediately went to the airport. There was a little photo booth there for taking passport photos. I had Angela get in, and I ran off four sets of photos. I would get them to my forger when I got back home. He would also get us visas and travel documents so we could travel about Vietnam. My forger was very well-connected, so all the needed documents would be on computers in Vietnam. But all this came at a price. If our plans went as we hoped, we would be back in Ho Chi Minh City within three weeks or month at the most. That would be late August, a nice time to visit Heaven. I thought to myself, it would be nice to have a few years in Heaven because I knew when I died that wasn't where I was going..

Chapter 27

◆

For over two weeks, the department's lawyers and the lawyers for the crew ships wrestled back-and-forth—precious time to lose that we wouldn't be getting back. We had to get things moving.

The cruise ships had joined forces blocking our warrants based on their fear of lost revenue and lawsuits from cruise passengers who had lost their lives. A couple of cruise lines were about to break ranks and agreed to help us out. Meaning giving us access to their data, but they were the older ones who only check passports against guest lists as people boarded. All of the big companies with the new technology of photos of passenger boarding and leaving were holding firm. And they were putting enormous pressure on the two about to break ranks and join us, so at the next meeting, they rescinded their pending agreement. Captain Colleen and I could attend all the negotiations. It was more frustrating than a blind man trying to analyze a crime scene.

Plus, we were having as much luck finding our three budding psychopaths as we were with the cruise line's lawyers and the lawyers for their insurance companies. We had two warrants issued, but they were being held up in appeals and could be there for months. During these times I was so glad I was in recovery.

I would've gotten lost in the bottle using these frustrations as excuses to have a drunken tantrum. One of Jim Syverson's famous lines kept coming back to me, "Excuses are just guarantees that you'll be making the same mistake again. There is no excuse for an alcoholic to drink." Kay was sensing my frustration, but instead of trying to fix it, she would just tell me to call my sponsor or go to a meeting or ask if there were some drunks I could help. But I also know that she was going to extra Al-Anon meetings. This behavior was such a big change for her. In the past, she would've been trying to take away my frustration. Believing she could and should make me happy to take away my troubles is what a good wife should do. I would just cling to them harder. They were my excuses to drink. But a small part of me longed for the days when she would've frantically been trying to make me feel better.

I talk to my sponsor. He just called it my alcoholic selfishness, that part of me that wanted more of something that wouldn't work and at Kay's expense. He also said it sounded like I was suffering from some self-pity. I was acting entitled, like everything should go my way. "Remember whoever you're chasing is fighting for his life though it is a sick, dangerous life. It's still his life. And he's fighting for its existence. Maybe you should take the wasted energy you're putting into the self-pity you're feeling and put that energy back into your work and Kay and Joey." He wasn't easy on me, but he was most often right that's why I respected and enjoyed him as a sponsor.

That night when Kay got home, Joey and I were in the kitchen with aprons on—fixing Joey's favorite meal, spaghetti with Italian meatballs---straight from our local Italian deli. There were also fresh flowers on the table. One of those small bottles of wine just enough for one or two glasses, the type we alcoholics think are useless but just enough for Kay. She looked at me, smiling. "Someone's been talking to their sponsor?"

I smiled. "Shut up, can a guy just do something nice for his wife? But Danny did have some helpful things to say and sends his greetings. He told me to recite the Serenity Prayer he felt it might apply."

"Let's say it as a family." Kay called Joey into the room. "Joey, would you like to say the Serenity Prayer with us?" We knew that he knew it. He heard it often from us and sometimes he would say it when we were putting him to bed. Kay told me her and Joey said it every night when I was out of the house.

The three of us held hands, "God grant me the serenity to accept the things I cannot change, the courage to change the things I can, and the wisdom to know the difference. Amen." Joey looked up at us. "I like doing this can we say that before meals? I think that would be nice." We all agreed and a new family ritual was born.

It was a delightful evening, and she sent Joey to bed early, for she had the twinkle in her eyes. After everything in the kitchen was cleaned up, she came to me playfully, "Bobby, I have a confession while you were gone all those years, I had an affair you know him." I had no idea where this was going, but I knew it would be fun and playful. "I've invited him here for a threesome tonight."

"Hmmm, who is this strange man?" Biting into her game.

"His name is Ricardo." She then pulled her vibrator out from behind her back. "Bobby, meet Ricardo!"

I was chuckling by now, "You named your vibrator?"

"Of course, it would be so impersonal if I didn't. Let's go to the other room, and you and Ricardo can pleasure me. I'm feeling selfish tonight." As we walked towards the bedroom, I just recited the Serenity Prayer out loud and Kay laughed.

"Prayer is probably be the only thing that going to save you tonight." We had a delightful, playful evening, which never would've happened if I've stayed in my self-pity and frustration.

The next day I got up a little bit early totally refreshed and went back to work with a different attitude. The same frustrations with there, but I was looking at them differently instead of roadblocks, they were merely challenges.

When Capt. Colleen came in, I sat her down and told her about a different strategy I had wanted to try. "It's risky, but I'd like to try calling their bluff. I think it's that Jamison fellow with the Waves of the Ocean cruise line who's the central linchpin. Doesn't it seem strange that he's the only CEO who comes to these meetings, the rest of them send senior vice presidents? I've been thinking about why he comes, not one of his flunkies. He seems to be the one that's got the lion share of power and appears to be blocking us the most. Me and Susan have done some research, and he has recently brought 4 million shares of stock in Waves of the Ocean before all this started. Plus, there are indirect talks of a merger.

So, if it came out, he'd take a hell of a hit. Sandy figured that the stock prices of all cruise lines would fall, easily fall 15%. The shares of Waves of the Ocean are trading at $119 a share. His shares alone are worth 476 million, and 15% haircut would mean he would lose 71 million with no guarantee of when the stock might recover. Plus, if he were counting on a bump in the share price from a favorable merger, that would be even more of a hit. I think we're dealing with old fashion greed.

He also looks at the age where he may be about to retire, and it would be a bad time for him to take the hit." I laid out the rest of my strategy to her and told her I knew she'd have to talk about it with those above us.

"No, Bobby, if we do this, I'm not going to be talking to them about it beforehand. I know that they would say no. This one's going to be on our heads, as they say, a career maker or a career breaker. If it doesn't fly, let's at least see if you and I can be partners on the beat down in the "No One Returns" section of town. The "No One Returns" was the nickname we had given to the worst and toughest area of Phoenix. It had the city's highest violence rate. A badge meant little, if anything, to the folks who frequented that part of town. Even cops didn't like being in that section of the city.

"So, you're willing to go for it?"

"Yeah, why not? What have we got to lose besides our careers? Let's not even tell the others I don't want Alex and Sandy taking the same risk."

"I agree. I absolutely agree."

At the next meeting with the cruise ship executives, their lawyers, our lawyers, I sat across from Mr. Randall Jamison, the CEO of Waves of the Ocean Cruise line. As the meeting got underway, Captain Colleen looked at Mr. Randall Jamison. "Mr. Jamison, something's been brought to our attention so Detective Collins and I would like to spend a couple of minutes with you alone. Would you be willing to give us 15 minutes of your time, just us and you off the record? He stared at us with an icy stare that would've made any detective proud, and we stared back at him with the same intensity. After about 30 seconds of seeing if he could get any indication from us on what this was about, he made his decision. "Absolutely, officers, I'm always willing to talk." Looking around, he just said, "Gentlemen, could you let us have the room for a bit. I'm sure this won't take long." Everybody was a bit confused and curious, but they got up and left, leaving myself and Capt. Colleen sitting directly across from our perceived adversary, the CEO of Waves of the Ocean Cruise Line. "Detective Collins, why don't you talk for us." Capt. Colleen was handing me the ball.

"Mr. Jamison, I'm going to read you two newspaper articles, one of which will, and I mean WILL be published tomorrow in the Phoenix Sun, the choice will be yours. We need to catch this man. He has killed at least 24 people known to us. We believe he's getting ready to kill more. But first, I want to see if I have my calculations right, you stand to lose somewhere in the range of 70-100 million dollars depending on what news comes out or it could be more. But I think there's a way where your stock could go up. I mean quite a bit more.

I read the first article.

Headline: "Phoenix Police Department are tracking a killer who hunts his victims on cruise lines, but they've run into a roadblock. Capt. Colleen Donahue and detective Bobby Collins told this reporter that they would have the suspect in custody by now. The only reason for the blockage of this vital information, which by the way, is readily available to the cruise lines they believe is for image reasons. But there may be another reason—pure and simple greed. The main blockage seems to be coming from what this reporter thought was a reputable and caring cruise line Waves of the Ocean. The main person who seems to be blocking the release of this information is Mr. Randall Jamison, the CEO of Waves of the Ocean Cruise line. He has recently bought 4 million shares of his company stock. Detective Collins thinks Mr. Jamison is personally blocking the investigation due to fear of personal financial losses if the news came out..."

"It goes on, but you get the gist of the article."
-Mr. Jamison stared at me and coldly said, "And the second article?"

Headline: "Phoenix police department with the help of Waves of the Ocean Cruise Line moves ever nearer to catching and apprehending a serial killer. Captain Colleen Donahue and Detective Bobby Collins told this reporter that with the generous help of Mr. Randall Jamison, the CEO of Waves of the Ocean Cruise Line and other cruise lines and their generosity and willingness to help in this ongoing investigation. The police department is very close to catching a serial killer that has been seeking out only high-end customers on various cruise lines as his victims. Under the leadership of Mr. Randall Jamison, the CEO of Waves of the Ocean Cruise Line, a group of the multiple cruise lines have been more than generous in helping to bring a dangerous person nearer to justice. Detective Bobby Collins, who was recently on a cruise with his wife. Said that he felt safe the whole time and even feels safer now knowing how much the entire cruise industry seems to care about their customers and their safety..."

"It goes on, but you get the gist of the article."

We stared at each other for a bit, then he said, "What is it that you want?"

We want full access to all of the passenger records on all of the different cruises, particularly the ones where photos were taken as passengers boarded. This so we can cross-reference and put everything together. We have a young super computer whiz Officer Sandy de Cotte we would like to have work with the people of your choosing. We think we can quickly identify our suspect. I can guarantee you that all we want and all that Officer de Cotte will leave that room with will be we'll be a file and hopefully a picture of one person. Again, only one person we don't care about any of the other passengers. Captain Colleen and I personally promise if you let us do this, the second article will run four days after we get our information whether we've apprehended him or not. But we want a little bit of a head start, using the information you will have given us.

"And if I don't agree?"

"I pressed the button on my computer. I guarantee you within five minutes, the reporter I'm sending this to will be calling asking their editor permission to run the story. You won't have time to kill it.

"You know you're risking your careers. You'll be out of a job."

"Actually, we've got a pretty good union, so we both think we will still have a job. It just may be walking the beat in the bad section of town." He smiled. "So, what's it going to be Mr. Jamison?"

"Oh, call me Randell and have that Officer de Cotte, I think you said Susan was her first name. Tell Susan to be ready to receive all of our tech people and their computers, no lawyers, tomorrow at ten sharply. I'm sure you have a secure room, it's a police department for god sake. The teams can work in it. Everybody will stay in that room except for secure bathroom breaks, which will be on that floor. Everyone stays there until you get your file. I don't care if it takes an hour or 10 days.

"You'll have full access to all of the cruise line records until you get what you need--one file. That's all you get. There will be one of our guards at the door checking that it's only one man's file. Now let's catch this son of a bitch. And if you don't mind, can I have a copy of that second article there are some ways I'd like to juice it up. Why don't we take a break you two can leave and get started on that secure room? I think your job is done here. Leave me with the others and the lawyers. I'll work everything out."

As he was walking away, he turned, "Two things! The first one and I will never admit to saying, "First, that second article will be good, especially after I spice it up. Plus, I would buy some of our stock before it comes out. You'll probably get about a 20% return on your money. Secondly, when you catch the son of a bitch. You and your families can have a free cruise on me with Waves of the Ocean Cruise Line and "Remind me never to play poker with you, Detective Collins." We all shook hands. He walked out of the room, and both Captain Colleen and I let out a big sigh of relief, "Captain, we did it, we did it!" "No, Bobby, you did it. Let's tell the others.

Back at the house, we brought Alex and Sandy in the room and told them all of the details. At first, they were, especially Alex mad, that we had not included them, "Why didn't you tell me I would've stood with you."

"That's exactly the point we knew both of you would've stood with us."

Sandy raised her hand, shaking it back-and-forth, "Well, I don't know about me, the rest of my career walking a beat down in the "No One Returns" section of town. Hey, I'm a lot younger than the rest of you, and to be honest, I do have flat feet. Thanks for not putting me on your bus."

I spoke up, "Well, the point is we did the math; two careers versus three or maybe four careers." I looked at Sandy. "The point is we got it and tomorrow we'll have all the information we need to break this case."

Capt. Colleen spoke up and with an ice-cold stare, looked at Sandy, "Okay, okay, we can hump on each other about what we should've done later, but we got to get ready for their people we've only got one shot at it. Little Miss Braveheart, this is your show from now on, and especially tomorrow, and you better shine."

I added, "We're going to set it up for all you nerds down in the basement. They're bringing their people and their computers and their data. You'll be allowed to walk out of there with one file and one name. So, you damn well better make sure it's the right one or you still may be spending most of your career walking the beat in the "No One Returns" section of town flat feet and all. So, what do you need from us?"

Sandy started barking out orders. Having us move everything that was in the conference room C down to the larger space in the basement. As we brought everything down, she reorganized and kept reorganizing it in ways that she thought she and the rest of the nerds could make more sense of it.

Capt. Colleen turned to me, "Bobby, can you do me a big favor, more than you already have, can you work late tonight and stay as long as we need you tomorrow? I know that's a lot to ask when you are working so hard to prove to Kay that she and Joey come before work. "Captain, I don't know, but I'll make the call. I want you standing right next to me and maybe talking to Kay so that she knows this is your idea, not mine."

"Absolutely, Bobby, absolutely."

I brought Kay totally up to speed with everything taking place, then swallowed and asked about working late both nights, Capt. Colleen grabbed the phone out of my hand. "Kay sweetie, I want you to know it's really me asking not Bobby he's made all the right calls so far and I need him at this juncture I know I'm asking a lot, but as one Al-Anon to another, it would be a big help. But I'm glad to see he has got his priority straight." I could hear Kay say, "Put Bobby back on."

"Honey, I just want you to know good going on the bluff."

"It wasn't a bluff, honey. I would've sent that first article."

"Well, no matter what, you are a good detective, a good husband, and father. Absolutely stay there as long as you need tonight, and tomorrow just nail this sonofabitch. I'll just spend the evening with Ricardo, it'll be like an old-time date but if you have any energy that you need to work off when you get home, wake me up. Or oh yeah, if you need to talk, just wake me up too. And by the way, thanks for asking first instead of just telling me that means a lot. Love you." I was shaking my head to let Capt. Colleen know that it was okay. She yelled out so Kay could hear her, "Thank you, Kay. I owe you."

Chapter 28

◆

Angela and I spent two days in the finest Singaporean hotel, mapping out the final details of our escape, walking the city, and making love. We both fell in love with the Singapore botanical gardens. We talked and fantasized about what type of plants to surround our home in Heaven with, Angela always told me how she wanted a large garden. She actually had some herbs growing in her little cabin on the ship. She got very involved in the plans for how to make our escape. She was very helpful and quickly understood what was needed and why. She was a bit disappointed but clearly understood why we needed to live in Ho Chi Minh City for a while, we needed to make sure that I hadn't been discovered and followed. She agreed that it was a good plan but a bit sad that it would take us some time to get to Heaven; it always does.

That morning from a street phone bank, I called my documents man up in Canada. I gave him the phone number of the phone next to me and told him to call me in five minutes on a phone he could talk from. Five minutes later, the phone rang. "Danny, (it wasn't his real name, names are always changed to protect the guilty). I'm married, and I'm going to get out of the business, but I'm going to need documents; two sets of passports for my new wife and myself.

"Congratulations, you finally found someone who will put up with your funky attitude. Okay, what are you thinking?" He always liked to get down to business.

"The original passports need to show us being from Canada; French Canadian."

He piped in, "Good, it's a good country. Not like your fucking country right now, its' a mess." He always was a bit political, but I didn't have time for that, so I went on.

"The second set needs to have us as citizens of Vietnam, French one of four languages she speaks fluently."

"Impressive, you found a classy lady and beautiful, I'm assuming?"

"Yes, but you'll see that in the pictures I'll be sending you. We're also going to need travel documents but have us hat Vietnamese citizens.. That's where we're going to end up disappearing, maybe!" I said with a chuckle.

"Interesting, good place to go get lost. You might see some of my customers there, but you would never know it. But it's going to make it easier for me. I know exactly what's needed. Thanks."

"What's your price?$150,000, for everything." I was a bit surprised.

"I was expecting double that." Why so generous?"

"Well, I'm going to be doing hers as a wedding present. The rest are at my normal prices with a little bit extra. You've been a good customer, and you never said anything the times when I overcharged you when I needed money. And truthfully, I think you will be back. You've got too much of a taste for it. And you're just too damn good at it."

"Thanks, but I'm going to be sending you an extra 25K because I need a rush job. I need it in a week. Can you do It?"

"A week, Jesus Christ, you're on the move."

"Yes"

"Yea, I can get it done, but it is going to mean some late nights. Here this information is for free, be careful there are rumors out there that they're getting close to taking someone big down. I don't know anyone more prominent than you. So maybe transfer the money right away. Danny laughed, but I knew he was dead serious.

"Do you know where the rumors are coming from?"

"All I know is that they're coming from down in the states, down in the southwest somewhere that's the best I can tell you. Just assume they're coming after you."

"I always have, Danny, I always have. I'm going to overnight her photos to you and have you send the package to the same place down in Seattle. I'm assuming monies wired to the same account, and I'll wire it when I get back to the hotel?" I'm ready for the address whenever you are."

In the years I've known him, I had never sent a package of work to the same address. He gave me an address in Vancouver where I assumed he lived. But I'd always wired the money to the same account in Switzerland. "You'll have them in a week. If I can get it done any sooner, I will, but I guarantee you I will meet your deadline, old friend."

"Thanks, Danny, thanks for everything." There was a tone of sadness we'd known each other for a couple of decades, and we both knew if things succeeded as we both hoped they would most likely this would be the last time we would ever talk with each other. We were thick as thieves, for that is what we both were.

"Congratulations, I bet she special. And again, I bet you'll be back!"

"Thanks! And she is." I didn't address his comment on me someday returning to the lifestyle. I wanted that question mark in his brain. It cost $429.50 to overnight the small bundle to Vancouver from Singapore. But money wasn't an issue---time was. From what Danny said I was going to be acting as if and assuming they were closing in on me so things would be moving fast.

That evening both Angela and I boarded the same plane to San Francisco, Angela in first class, and I far back in the economy section. From there, she would go to Colorado to see her mother and grandmother. I sat in the rear of the plane in case they were onto me. She would be gone, and she wouldn't have to witness what would happen if they try to take me alive. We had agreed to no contact on the flight, and when she got off the plane, she would not wait for me. She would go on to her next flight and her final visit to her mother and grandmother. Our having no contact, even visual, it was more for her protection than mine. If they were onto me and we got off the plane and talked with each other or even looked at each other, she would immediately be tagged as connected to me. I knew how to stay away from cameras, but she didn't, and why should she, that wasn't her world."

We would meet up once in Seattle, Washington, to give her the diamonds and for their insertion. Then she would depart from there back to Singapore with a new passport. She would vacation for a couple of days before reinserting her packages and flying on to Vietnam. I would drive down to San Francisco and leave directly to Vietnam and Ho Chi Minh City and look for two apartments. One apartment we would live in daily. Hopefully, the second we would never live in it, it would be there with items I would need if we had to make some type of escape. I was pretty sure if we made it to Vietnam, these precautions would not be needed. The rule I lived by: precautions must always be taken hopefully never used. Things would be moving fast these next days, and I liked that; I was sharper during those times. I would take Danny's advice and just assume that they were a step ahead of me or stepped behind me all the time. My final hunt was on.

In less than 24hours after landing, I was standing ringing the doorbell of Randell Tang. I knew they would be home by then. I had disarmed his alarm system so neither the security company nor the police would be notified. He was stunned, "Mr. Ray, what are you doing here?"

"I have an exceptional business proposition I wanted to offer and talked to you about but not on the boat. I'm so sorry to intrude on you

197

like this, but I wanted to talk to you about it before I headed home. It could make you lots and lots of money, and me too, of course.

From a distance, I could hear Ivana, "Who's here."

Randell shop back, "Mr. Ray from the ship?" Ivana came in from the other room a bit startled. When I saw that neither one of them had a cell phone in their hand, I acted like I was going to shake their hands, and I used my Taser and zapped both of them to the ground. Even before the shaking had stopped, they were both bound in zip ties.

"Now Randell, I want to see that Titan 1200-XR. It's in the study, if I remember correctly."

I dragged both of them into his study. Their cell phones were lying on the top of the counter. "I'm assuming you keep it in your study so that it's close to you. What's the combination." "I'm not going to tell you!" He yelled at me defiantly.

"Yes, you will! Nobody's ever refused; it's just money, and I know you've got lots more in other places. What's the combination and I want the combination to the safe in your bedroom too. The one where Ivana's jewels are kept, this was some information that had come out over cognac and cigars after a poker game. Randell had won $10,000 from me. He had a pair of aces, and I had a full house. He always talked more when he won.

"Dammit, I told you I'm not going to tell you the security folks will be here soon. I would leave if I were you."

"Not really, I disconnected everything before I rang your doorbell. I thought you might be like this." I grabbed Ivana, placed her in a chair, got out a scissor cut off the buttons of her blouse, and opened it up, and cut off her bra. She was sitting there bare-chested. I couldn't help myself. I reached out and grabbed one, "Just like I thought, they're not real." Randell being the ass he was yelled out, "But real expensive." I then got out my Cream Brulé torch and fired it up. "Now tell me the combination, or I'm going to hurt her really bad. I will start with these fake boobs until one of them pops." Her eyes were going crazy, and she was begging for mercy through the gag I put on her. "I'm going to ask you one more time what is the....

He interrupted me, "I don't give a shit. Do what you want to her I can always get another."

She was looking at him with pure hatred. I then took the gag off her, "Do you know the combination to the safe?" The combination for the downstairs safe is 14-25-7, and the combination for the upstairs safe is 27-10-52. The safe in the bedroom upstairs works, but the safe down here doesn't work; he needs to get it fixed.

"So, Ivana, I take it. He never told you that the safe down here has to be activated with eye recognition. Then you enter the combination. It's programmed only for his eyes, not yours. I bet it works perfectly."

She looked at him with hatred. "You son of a bitch, You son of a bitch."

"Here's the thing, Ivana. I'm going to need your help. "I'm going to put more zip ties on your ankles, so don't even think about running, then I will undo your hands. Then I'm going to bring your husband and stand him in front of the safe. I'll hold his face steady close to the safe, but I'll need his's eyes opened real wide. So, I want you to pull down his pants and take this little torch and hold it to his balls, I'm sure his eyes will be wide-open then, and we'll both get to see what he has kept from you." There was no objection from her. Soon I could smell burning flesh and hear screams as I had never heard before. I heard a click that meant the combination could now be entered. I pushed him to the side. He fell to the ground, not going anywhere because of the zip ties.

It was clear to all of us I didn't need him anymore. Ivana kept the torch on his balls and prick, "This is for all the times you made me suck this little thing in front of your friends and let me be their plaything." The door swung open she didn't even seem to care what was behind the safe's door. She was too busy getting revenge for all the indignities he had put

199

her through. The contents of the safe were better than I thought or dare dream of. There must've been at least $1 million in US currency and another million-plus in euros and lots of gold. I counted 20 kg of gold. He didn't bother with silver. Ivana was busy with her work, a big revengeful smile on her face, and he was screaming into his gag. I asked her, "What the combination to the upstairs safe. "27-10-52" It was the same number she had given me earlier. There was no need for them anymore. I took out my gun and put two rounds in his head so she could watch. She smiled. Then I put two bullets in her head. Their lives were over. I blew out the torch and put it back in my kit. I then quickly made it upstairs and to their bedroom. Companies that install safes are always so predictable. I swung aside the picture, the only one on the walls, and behind it was the safe. It opened quickly.

There were plenty of beautiful diamond necklaces, brooches. There was even a small outfit made out of strings of medium grade diamonds. It would wrap around her breasts with another three strands of diamonds hanging down to just above her womanhood framing it. She must have been on display often to his friends, to show off her beauty, his wealth, and his complete power and control over her. There were more diamonds in her jewelry than I made in the past to two burglaries together.

A thought came. There was only dollars, euros, and gold in the safe below. Where were his traveling diamonds? These were his show off diamonds. Did he have another safe? Had I made a mistake and killed him too soon?

I gathered up all the jewelry, threw them in the bag, and headed back downstairs to the safe. I packed up all the treasures but was also pounding around. Then I heard a hollowness. I lifted up what was a false bottom and there was a compartment and another pouch. I smiled. I knew what it was. I pulled it out and poured the pouch's contents onto the desk. It was filled with high-quality uncut diamonds, probably from the blood mines of Africa. All were at least a carat in size, most more like three or four carats, plus there were many perfectly cut diamonds, all at least two carats in size many larger. Randell and Ivana, we're giving me the best wedding present I could ask for---diamonds lots of diamonds.

Underneath the pouch were pictures of Ivana being used sexually by large gatherings of men. It quickly became apparent that he would have his friends over to use her all at once. In one picture, I counted 15 guys. There were before and after photos. In the after pictures, Ivana looked rough, really rough, and used up. It was clear they hadn't been easy with her. It now made so much sense why she was having such a good time with the torch. My only regret was that I couldn't have given her more time. She was rolling him over, probably to do ugly things to him when I put the bullets in their heads. My time was more precious than her fun.

I loaded everything up to the van I had bought with cash earlier that day. I used that dealership where you could do the paperwork right there, not needing to go to any county office. Or even provide accurate information; all you needed was papers that looked like papers and cash. Every town has one.

It took two trips to bring my treasures to the van. I kept thinking to myself there's enough here to build heaven and live there forever. Unknowingly he had saved the Dohm's lives. There would be no need for a second burglary and murder. I went into the house, cleaned it as thoroughly as I could. The only evidence I left was the Cream Brulé torch. After finding the pictures, I had put it back in her hand. She looked so happy holding it. I threw the photos I found on top of the two of them. Maybe making the police think it was a sex crime/robbery. There was no taking them to their beds. There was no mint left on the pillow. There was just a lifetime of misery and death lying on the floor in front of his safe.

I was out of their mansion back in my van heading north cruise control set at the posted speed limit heading home to start gathering treasures and condensing them down. My treasures from all these years would be providing Angela and me with 'da very good new life.

I made several stops along the way, gathering up everything from the many different spots where did been kept secretly. Again, the gun was thrown in a lake. There was only one person I knew of that I could call to

201

exchange the gold and silver and jewelry pieces for more top-grade diamonds. I called him, we never use names, but he instantly recognized me. I gave him a number of a burner phone.

And he called me back in five minutes. "It's moving day, my friend."

I heard joy on the other end. "Oh my God, I've been waiting for this day. Hallelujah, and congratulations, are you going to South America, Africa, Europe, hell, you never tell me anyway, but congratulations. What are you thinking?"

I said, "Thirteen for ten," that should be fair. All untraceable gold, silver, jewelry, and cash too much for me to take."

"Thirteen for 9," he shot back.

I answered, "Thirteen for 9.4, all super high-quality large caret."

"Deal!" I had tallied it up and I actually had approximately $20 million that I would be exchanging with him for diamonds. As I gave him the numbers, and he just laughed and said, "Hell with these numbers, 9.5." We settled on $15,500,000 in diamonds. Not a bad day for him and I would have what I needed. So, with the diamonds I would be getting from him, plus the ones I already had and the money I would be sending over to different hotels, Angela and me would be able to start a new life with approximately $20 million. And with where we were going, we would live like gods.

We set up the meet, and I added, "Bring your packing machine." "I always do. I hope your ass can handle it all.

I went to my home through the tunnels to where I kept my journals that someday would be my legacy with the police. I wanted no traces of my old life left behind. I threw them in the fireplace and burnt them. Angela would now be my legacy. I had no regrets.

I spent the night before the meet, packing the euros I would be sending to the five hotels in Ho Chi Minh City. My Canadian document guy had given me the hotel names of them and what and how to pack the currency. If only three were waiting for me, that would still be good starting money.

My diamond man showed up at the designated time. He was as satisfied as was I. All together, when done packaging things up, we had 25 one and a half inch bundles, each worth a small fortune. Each made up of high-quality diamonds he was exchanging with me for my gold, silver, extra cash, and jewelry pieces I had stolen over the years. We mix the diamonds he was giving me with the ones I already possessed and package them up. As we were leaving, he went to his small truck that had extra, extra duty suspension on it to handle the weight of the gold. He came back. "A little present for you. It'll help." It was a jar of KY lubrication. "Good luck, my friend, good luck I hope you may find your little piece of heaven and they never find you."

Then he handed me his real going away present. It was a list of initials and phone numbers. Three sets of initials and three sets of phone numbers for each continent. "Wherever you're going, and I don't want to know, these are people I trust with my life. I've worked with them for years. They will help you turn the diamonds into local currency. Never give them more than 8%. They'll start at 20% but never give them more than eight. Use my name if needed."

We shook hands, each then going our separate ways. I went back to my home, translated the initials into numbers in my unique code, and through the sheet of paper he'd given me into the fire. I scribbled hard on a piece of paper a name and a time crumpled it up, placed it behind the logs to be used in the fireplace. It looked as if it had been thrown into the fire but didn't quite make it., I also left the pad on a small table near the fireplace with a burner phone lying next to it. I threw the rest of my papers into the fire rub-down the entire place and was on my way to Seattle to meet up with my wife. I love twisting my wedding band as I drove.

203

Chapter 29

That morning at precisely 10 o'clock, a small army of geeky looking men and women walked through the station following the signs that pointed to the basement. Thank goodness they put it in the basement. Each of the cruise lines had sent a pair of their tech experts. There was barely room for everyone and their equipment. Sandy stood up was about to say something when an executive type interrupted her, "Officer de Cottle, if I may say a word or two first."

Not even waiting for a response, he said, "I'm Mr. Bill Vain, Vice Pres. in charge of operations of Waves of the Ocean Cruise Line." Puffing his chest out a bit. "I am Mr. Randall Jamison's the CEO of Waves of the Ocean Cruise Line second in command. Also, all of your CEOs of the other cruise lines have authorized me to speak for them. Our client's personal data is of our utmost importance. When I'm done talking, a security agent from each of your specific companies will hand out a company owned and secure computer. These computers have each of your company's specific information on them, use only the computers given to you by your company security representative. The same security representative will be here when we end to collect the computers. I needn't remind you, but I will, the security of our client's personal data is of our utmost importance.

"Now we are here to catch a serial killer. This man does his hunting, looking at Susan. "That is the correct word, isn't it, 'hunting', Officer de Cottle?" She shook her head in agreement. "On our cruise lines, he hunts, and then in their homes robs and kills his victims. A despicable man! Today, Officer de Cottle will be in total charge, so if something goes wrong, it falls on her." He chuckled, "just kidding," but everybody got his message. "When I'm finished speaking, whatever, and I mean whatever, she tells you to do, you do it. If you think you have a good idea or something that may help the task at hand, run it by officer Sandy de Cottle; she's the pro. Please, even though we are competitors outside this room here today, we are a team, work as a team, one purpose, one purpose only to catch this guy. All cell phones will now be deposited in the baskets with your names on them. It is crucial, and I mean, crucial that no information about what is transpiring here is communicated to anyone outside of this room. The media would have a field day, and he, this killer would get the upper hand. You will be staying in here until this is finished if any of you choose to leave before then consider yourselves unemployed. I don't care if it takes all night or two nights or two months, we're going to catch this guy. All meals will be catered into the room. There are bathrooms across away, but you're not allowed to leave this floor. You can imagine what this would and will do to our industry if this man is not caught." Remembering to be politically correct, he added, "The detectives have assured me that they're sure it's a man and not a woman. We all know women could be killers too. I've been assured we are not dealing with some petty criminal here. He is a pro. How many of you have seen Silence of the Lambs?" Every hand in the room when up, "Well, it does scare me a bit the detectives assure me that he is as smart and as deadly as 'Hannibal the Cannibal.' The only difference he doesn't eat his victims, at least not that we know of. But we have a room of Penelope Garcias, not even stopping because of his last reference." He kept going. It was becoming clear to let Mr. Vain, go on who clearly watched a lot of cop movies and cop shows and was enjoying his day at the house would not be helpful. Sandy coughed loudly to let him know he had gone on way too long. This group of millennials were drifting, thank goodness he got the message. Everyone was sure he could've gone on for another 10 minutes. "Okay, folks, let show him that we're smarter than him."

Sandy got up and introduced herself and using all of her geek type language explained to them all that she had done. How she had organized the walls and what she believed needed to take place as company officials were handing out computers to their employees. To bring them back to focus after Mr. Vain's ramblings, Sandy pointed to the walls. She knew she needed visuals with this group. "I don't know if any of you have ever seen real crime scene pictures, they're not pretty but surrounding you are the pictures of what all he has done to his victims, your customers. Some of the people instantly and intensely started looking at the photos. Others were looking away. "Feels free at any time to wander around, looking at the data we have gathered so far. Underneath each picture of a victim is critical information we have accumulated about each crime scene. Please study them look for patterns. I know on the TV shows and movies that Mr. Vain referenced, they always get the guy within an hour. We've been at these for months, but finding out he's been hunting his victims on cruise lines is the best break we've had yet. I believe that within hours, a day, or two, we can identify who he is with our detective skills, your data, and expertise. Sandy introduce Bobby, Alex and Captain Colleen, very briefly." And then went on spewing out details and data none of us understood but they were eating it up.

One young gentleman raised his hand. "If I can say every one of these victims is in the eight or nine-digit category of wealth. I think that means that we can automatically rule out two cruise lines they don't cater to that clientele Carnival and Royal Caribbean. He looked over at those representatives. "No offense."

"None taken." The representative from Royal Caribbean added, "But we have few hundred maybe a thousand or two people on our list that would fit that wealth category. I'll enter them into the central computer." She bent down and tapped keys. The room quickly came alive with questions, answers, and ideas being thrown around quicker than a squirrel on amphetamines. People were up looking at the pictures, pointing things out, yelling at someone with a computer to check on something. One fellow yelled out, "Who are these three?" The room went quiet for a second, and Sandy took a bit of time to explain the three child psychopaths, their stories, their backgrounds, and why they were up on the boards and how they might be connected. Then another person yelled out, "Okay, got it, thanks, let's get going again." The whirlwind of activity continued around one in the afternoon food was brought in the operations slow down a bit but not much.

About 11:30 p.m., someone yelled, "Bingo, our guy's name is Daniel Ray" More importantly, on the screen was a picture of him as he appeared on each cruise. "He tries to alter his face as much as he can, especially on the short cruises, but this is him. He's finding his guys playing poker, and he is a dam good poker player."

Everybody was staring at the picture, another guy yelled out, "I think he's one of your three kids" Using facial recognition. I went through all pictures of him from the cameras we have on our ship. "Look at this one." He popped up a picture of the man first called Daniel Ray, stepping out of the pool on the ship. The guy blew up the image of his arm, and there was a scar at least 8-inches long on his right arm. "What arm did that kid cut?" Someone yelled out, "His right one." The same person yelled out, "His birth name is Benjamin Thatch, September 5, 1974, in and Sandy yelled out New Smyrna Beach, Florida. More information started being thrown out. Someone started putting together a timeline of the foster homes he had gone through. He has been suspected of being involved as a male prostitute in his youth." Someone else yelled out "The two foster home parents he lived with the longest were both charged with and convicted of sexually abusing children in their care.

"I may have his first kill," a young woman yelled out. "In Orlando, a man was found murdered. A butcher knife through the heart, the guy, had a history of picking young boys and being awfully rough with them. The guy was stabbed, and from everything we can tell, the kid hung around watching TV, showering and making himself something to eat. Then he robs the house of any of its valuables." Bobby, amazed and gleeful about what was happening, yelled out, "Jesus Christ, where the hell are you getting this information?" Three or four of them simultaneously yelled, "Don't ask!" Then another guy yelled out, "But congratulations on your 3+ years of sobriety." Another young lady yelled out, "Next time when you and your wife take a cruise, please fill out the survey with more detail, and you sure ate of the 24-hour buffet quite a bit, thank you very much."

Someone else yelled out, "Sorry to see your wife is buying a lot of sex toys. Bobby shot back, "And I hope she buys more!" The whole room laughed. Susan said, "Back to Mr. Thatch, we can grade Detective Collin's sex life later. But thank you dam good work!" Over the next few hours, they have put together a good picture of who Benjamin Thatch was his trail of aliases. They even had a picture of him caught on a traffic camera about 10 miles away from Gil and Mary Deutsch's two days before they were murdered, when he took off his hat briefly.

The dominoes were falling quickly. After about another hour, because the whole group could now be focused on one specific person, they had narrow down to where Daniel Ray lived in Hayden Lake, Idaho. Detective Collins phoned up to Coeur d' Alene to a detective Samuelson. Someone he had known for years to explain the situation and asked him to drive up and try and take him, "and Sammy if he's there. He us a bad one that..." detective Samuelson interrupted him, "I get the drift buddy I get the drift." I'll call you back in an hour or two. Bobby swore he could hear sirens in the background even before he hung up. The entire group sat there on pins and needles eating and resting. The room was as intense as Houston's mission control as everyone waited for the Apollo 11 to land on the moon.

After a two and 15 minutes, the phone rang. "Bobby, the place is empty. Our forensic guys are just starting to work on it now, but they can't find a damn print anywhere. The fireplace is full of ashes. A bunch of something had been burned. The only thing we found was a crumpled-up piece of paper behind the woodpile next to the fireplace it looked as if someone tried to throw it in the fireplace and it bounced behind the woodpile." Detective Samuelson read what was on the paper.

Suddenly, someone in the room yelled out, "Jesus Christ, that's one of our clients who was on a ship with this guy not long ago.

On the note there was also a day and a time given, "Christ he's going to kill and rob them in two days." Alex yelled out, "No, he's not we will be there and nail him, we've got him. We're going to catch him red-handed." A cheer went up throughout the room. Over the next two hours, everybody packed up and put the information together into one complete file.

Someone even stood up and made a small speech about how proud it was to be a part of this, and now was time to turn the real work back over to the detectives. Everybody was singing Sandy's praise for the way she had been directing and leading everybody for these past 18 hours.

Sandy stood up. "Thanks, everyone! We knew we would find the answer in your data. BUT please, and I beg you not a word to anyone until he is in custody. We have no idea where he has eyes and ears. We don't want to alarm him. We got one chance at this. Bobby thinks we should keep you all here until we've got him, but I trust you'll be quiet. You don't want your good work to be in vain. And we've got two lives to save. Loose lips sink ships."

One by one, they were walking out of the room. The guard was giving them back their cell phones. The representative from each of the cruise lines was collecting up the computers that their company personnel had used. All the geeks were leaving with big smiles on their faces. They were real crime fighters. One young lady came up to Sandy, "Don't be startled with what I do next the guard will see me." The young woman who was about Sandy's age then reached into Sandy's blouse put her hand inside Sandy's bra, tapping her breast but leaving a piece of paper. She then turned sensuously smiling and walked past a guard, "What was that do I need to search her? I was leaving her my phone number. She's gay like me. We've been flirting with each other all day. I wanted to do that since this thing started yesterday morning. If you do have to search her, let me hang around I can do a more thorough job than you can." The guard just motioned her on.

When the room was empty except for Sandy, Alex and Bobby, Sandy took out the folded-up piece of paper the girl had left in her bra. I know we're only supposed to do one person, one file. But I think the girl who skinned her brother's dog is Angela Addison living in Colorado Springs, Colorado, and she may be responsible for these five murders. The note listed their names. Susan had noticed this particular girl had been quiet the whole time intensely working on something. She didn't interact with the others much. Now Sandy knew what she had been doing. The note read, "I knew the others would find him, so I went another direction. I hope this helps. Thank you for your good work! This was fun! signed G."

Chapter 30

◆

Everything was ready, and I was so excited to see Angela, but she didn't arrive at the prescribed time. She had always been so precise about everything before. Two hours past and still, my wife was not there. Something was wrong. Did she get cold feet? Did she go to the police? Did they catch her? My mind was frantically searching for answers. None were to be found. I've been made a fool by falling in love, it had never done me any good in the past. Then I had to remind myself I have never been in love before, just lust.

I needed to get busy. I was crazy nervous. I made a couple of calls. I checked out the rumors with others I knew, and they had heard the same thing the police were looking to take somebody big down. I had a friend with a contact in the Police Department that for a price information could be gotten. I called him, "Percy, I need more information on the rumors how much?"

"This is big stuff that's kind of means big-money. $6000 for me and $5000 amongst my contacts."

"Ouch! And I need it quick."

"Then let's make it an even $15,000, and you'll have the information from me in four hours."

"Let me know if there's any word about a woman in the rumors."

Four hours later, I was out walking around one of the Lakes when Percy called my burner phone. "There are no names, but it has to do with

211

a serial killer. The police have been arguing with lawyers for the cruise lines wanting information. The cruise lines worried about their image are withholding right now to a stalemate. It's all taking place down in Phoenix."

"Do you know who the lead detective is?"

"Yes, yes, I was just getting to that; those are the type of details you pay me for. The lead detectives on this are a Detective Collins and a Detective Hollander out of the main Phoenix house. There is some talk which I can't confirm yet the rest of what I'm giving you. But the rumor is at the stalemate it's about to break. There is no mention of a woman." As Daniel was getting back into his car, Percy asked, "Is this about you?"

"No, much to my relief, but with what you're telling me, but I know who to call and relay this information to, and I'll get my 15,000 back plus a bit more. I'm pretty sure I know who they're talking about and he'll pay handsomely. You are not the only one in the information business."

Though Percy had always been reliable and discreet, his business was that of selling information, so I didn't want to give him the information that it was about me. I didn't know how close they were getting, but he was letting me know two things. First, they were on to me, and second, they were damn close. Dam that detective Collins, he was good; he had made the connection to the cruise ships. Me, my ego and that stupid mint. The answers I got from Percy bought me a few more hours, and right now, time was of the essence.

Where was Angela? I was frantic. I kept going back to where we were to meet. I didn't know if she remembered that we had said if something happened and either of us for late, we would meet on the hour. It was a casual comment I had made as we were going over so many details; it's something that could've easily been forgotten or not heard. But she had been late for over 12 hours.

Had they gotten to her? Maybe she's been working with them all along? Maybe I should have killed her? My fears were activating all my

212

animal instincts survival thoughts were re-emerging? I could feel that part of me wanting to be in control. My animal wanting me give up on love it was making fun of me, telling me what a fool I had been to even believe there could be love for someone like me. My brain was reminding me of those who had said they love me in the past and then hurt me. I so didn't want to add her to that list. I truly believe she was different, but I have been wrong in the past, maybe again. With what Percy had told me, I knew I had limited time. I decided I would wait for 24 hours and that if she was not there. I would seek my own survival. Now I so wished I haven't burnt my journals. Now my legacy was probably just going to be another fool who believed in love and got burned. I still reminded myself I would not go quietly into the night.

The 24 hours had come and gone. My soul, if I had one, was crushed, I started putting my steel coat around my heart again. "One more fucking hour." About 25 minutes later, there walking down the path and then running when she saw me was Angela. I ran to her. She was crying.

"Oh, my darling, I'm so sorry I'm late three days before I got home, my grandmother died. I had to wait and bury her. She was the only other person besides you that's truly loved me. I couldn't leave her to my mother, who was off getting drunk and seeking solace in the arms of some stranger who would buy her whiskey; the ticket into her pants. I was so scared you wouldn't be here. I would've understood. I'm sorry, I had to stay and bury her, I just had to stay and bury her." Her whole body was shaking.

I hugged her, trying to reassure her that everything was alright. The animal inside me was disappointed that it was going to be pushed down again, at least for now. "No time honey! We have to go things are moving fast, the detectives I told you about are starting to put things together. We'll talk in the car. I'm doing everything I can to buy us time, but there's not much of it. Men are chasing me, and now you. The issue now is time. My hunting days are over and now we are being hunted."

I had wanted to show her my cabin, but there wasn't time, we started driving to Seattle. Angela needed to talk. "I'm so, so, sorry I'm late. I had to bury her. Someone who loved her had to be there. I hadn't told you the whole truth I told you that both my mother and grandmother were good people it was only a half-truth. At one time, my mother was a good woman. Then my father abandoned her. It crushed her heart. I was only five. After some time, she started taking refuge in the bottle and the beds of strangers. One night when my mother had given this new man what he wanted, she passed out. I woke up to see him with the evilest face I'd ever seen standing in my doorway, bracing himself using the sides of the frame. He took a step into the doorway. The evil in his eyes got worse. 'Your mother was good, but you're fresh innocence.' He didn't see her, but my grandmother was sitting in a rocking chair in the corner. She pulled on the small chain of the lamp. That was on my nightstand. The tiny light somewhat illuminated the room. But now it was enough for him to see my grandmother sitting there with a 12-gauge shotgun being raised from her lap. 'Child close your eyes. Close your eyes right now. I'm going to give this scoundrel two choices. I'm not sure which one he will choose because it's clear he's used to making bad choices. He's with your mother.' I close my eyes. 'Sir, you have two choices; First back out of this room, leave our home and never come back; Second, and truthfully I hope you choose it. You can take one more step forward towards my granddaughter, and you can be burning in hell within moments. Choose wisely, I never miss.' The man slowly backed out of the room, and soon I heard our front door slamming behind him.

"That next morning when my mother woke with a hangover, she said, "Where is my boyfriend? I like him?"

I told her, "Mommy he came into my room last night he looked terrifying he wanted to do something to me calling me fresh meat I didn't like that. Grandma was there with her gun he left I don't think he's coming back."

My mother looked at her mother, "Why did you interfere? I liked him. I knew if you hadn't interfered, he would've stayed with me for a while.?"

My grandmother got up. She walked over to her and slapped her so hard she went flying onto the ground. "If you ever bring a man like him

214

to our house again, remember there are two barrels to my shotgun." Every night when my mother would go out, my grandmother would sit in the corner of my room with her shotgun on her lap until I was old enough to have one of my own. Daniel, she was my first protector I had to be there for her." She was wiping away her tears.

I reached out and grabbed one of her hands and squeezed it. "I understand, honey. I would've done the same. Angela relaxed. I put on some music. Nice soft, soothing music.

Down the road, she said, "Can't you drive faster if time is important?" "When you have the cargo that we are carrying, one never goes over the speed limit or gives the police any reason for them to stop them. She smiled. I turned off the radio. "Please sing that song that your grandmother used to sing to you. I would like to hear it again." The sweet melody filled the car until we were back feeling connected, back being husband-and-wife---husband and wife on the run.

On the hour we turn the radio on listening to the top of the hour news, nothing was being said. I didn't think there would be any news until there was some type of conclusion but gave us something to do on the drive.

We got to Seattle and checked into the hotel. "Now, honey, I've got your tickets, but we must get you ready for your flight. Your flight leaves in seven hours. I will crossover and fly from Vancouver.

Do you remember what hotel you go to when you're in Singapore?"

"The Singapore Hyatt."

"Perfect, there will be a room booked for you empty the contents and put them in the safe, then enjoy the next couple of days it will be the last time we have to be apart. Don't undo any the packages you'll need to put them back in your storage compartments. I've already tested them. No metal detectors in any airport will be activated. Now get undressed and lay on the bed."

Angela smiled, actually giggling. "Compartments what a funny name. How about you make love to my compartment before we fill it with those," she said, pointing at the diamonds, "Besides, it'll be nice to know there's a little bit of you up been there with them." We made love much quicker than we normally would have, but I think it helped relax her. I put some packets up inside her vagina. She patted her little triangle, "my million-dollar pussy." "Honey Randell had more gifts for us than I thought he would, it's more like up two-million-dollar kitten, but you need to rollover. She rolled over, and the end of an anal plug was staring at me. She looked over her shoulder at me.

"Nothing has ever been up there that wasn't supposed to be there before. But I've seen these things in some of the drawers and nightstands of some guests on the cruises. I know what they were for; I thought it would help get me ready."

It helped considerably. Angela had some discomfort, but nine packages vanished up inside her backside more easily than either of us expected. She walked around the room nude at times jumping up and down to see if anything would fall out. Nothing did. She was getting used to how it felt, and I was staring at this beautiful woman going through weird movements thinking that's is my wife. She motioned to the anal plug that had been up her backside, "Do you want to use it until it's time for your flight you got more to put up than me?"

I told her, "No, but thanks. I've had to do this before only with drugs, which is much more dangerous. I gave her a dozen condoms and told her she knew where to get more if any of the packages broke. First to wrap the diamonds in paper and then wrap each package with three condoms tying them tight and cutting off let ends. I had her try once she did precisely what was needed. I gave her, her passport, and I kept the other one, and I gave her one of my passports and kept the other one. We spent an hour going over details. Then we got ready, and I took her and her luggage to the Seattle airport. I got out of the car to give her a big hug and kiss. I didn't want to let her go, even if it would be for only five days. Because of the delay, there were some doubts in my head. I worked to

216

push aside, but I did wonder if I would ever see her again. I think she sensed it, she grabbed my face and kissed me intensely. "In five days, we will never be apart again, I will be there on time there is no one left bury."

I watched her walk away, not knowing if I was the luckiest man in the world or the biggest fool.

I then headed north to the border. I wanted to get in the evening traffic of people going home into Vancouver. That's where my passports said I was from. But I had one stop to make it would be a quick million dollars. It went pretty smoothly with the customs agent, only asking me one trick question. It was one that most anyone from Vancouver would know. "You live up near the Yaletown. How's that new development going? It's supposed to be a pretty damn big deal."

"Oh, you mustn't have heard we all got together and blocked it, yes, yes it would've created some jobs, but it would've killed the character of our neighborhood we just couldn't let it happen."

He smiled and nodded. "I would've been on the same side of the fences as you on this one, sometimes progress must be stopped or at least thought out better than this one was." I agreed with him. We would talk some more, but the car behind me honked, "Some anxious person wanting to get home. You have a pleasant night."

"Sir, you too." I was supposed to be on a flight heading straight to Ho Chi Minh City in five hours. There was still one hurdle to be jumped. But maybe I would let it pass.

Chapter 31

◆

Alex and I were with the sniper. The sniper knew the shot had to be precise. A civilian would be close sometimes right in front of him. We were waiting for the Chief of Police Stan Maysack to give his okay. But something seemed off to me. Alex, who was to provide the signal heard in his earpiece. The Chief was giving everything the green light. "Okay, go ahead if you got the shot, but for God's sake, don't hit the civilian."

Alex yelled to the sniper, "Shoot!"

Just as the sniper was pulling the trigger, I pushed the rifle away, yelling, "No, it's not him; it's not him."

A shot rang out, and I saw Mr. Paul Tieden fall to the ground, grabbing his ear. The ceramic tile behind him shattered into 1000 pieces flying in every direction. The delivery man fell to the ground, his hands flailing as he tried to crawl to the bushes as if the shrubs would stop a high caliber bullet.

Mr. Tieden's wife Susan fell to the ground, screaming as some officers yelled, "Police don't move or you're dead, don't move."

Everything for a second or two became still as rocks, but the crying and the whimpering filled the air Mr. Tieden started yelling, "I've been shot. I've been shot help. Please get me some help."

Susan, Paul's wife, risking life and limb yelled, "I'm his wife. I'm going to him don't shoot, don't shoot." She then ran to her husband, cradled his head in her lap, trying to offer some comfort and stop the bleeding.

Neither of them was able to make sense of what had just happened as 35 police in full gear ran, converging on the house their guns at the ready.

Alex, the sniper, and I ran from where we were to the front of the house. I yelled at the deliveryman. He was lying on his stomach in the bushes, shaking, "Rollover, you sonofabitch." He did, and his cap rolled off in the process. I instantly knew it wasn't our guy. "SHIT! SHIT! SHIT! SHIT!"

He had wet himself. The delivery man just laid there, shaking, crying. "I didn't do anything, don't kill me. I was just delivering a package. I don't even know what's in it or who they are. I didn't do anything why do you want to kill me please I was just hired to deliver a package please don't shoot." The stain between his legs was getting bigger.

I went over to Mr. Tieden put my hand on his shoulder. "We'll get you some help right away but first do you know this man?" I held out our picture of Benjamin Thatch.

"Yes," barked out Susan Tieden holding her hand over her husband's ear to try and stop the bleeding, yelled out, "That's Daniel Ray he was on the cruise my husband and me were just on."

Paul spoke up, "Excuse my language, I'm normally a civil man, but what the fuck is going on here why did you shoot me and not him pointing at the delivery man."

Knowing that this was going to be the colossal fuck up of the century, Bobby started trying to manage the situation. "This man here this Daniel Ray, he actually is Benjamin Thatch, a dangerous serial killer who has killed over twenty people. You were going to be his next victims. We had good intel and reason to believe he was on his way to kill and rob you and Susan. We thought the deliveryman was him.

"So why did you shoot me? Is your guy a lousy shot?"

The sniper standing next to Bobby spoke up, "No, I'm a dam good shot I would've hit him if he hadn't pushed my barrel at the last second." The blame machine was already being turned on.

Bobby looked at him. "Go to the truck."

"But."

"Go to the truck."

"After the order had already been given to shoot, I realized the delivery man was too young to be Daniel Ray. I pushed the barrel of the gun away; unfortunately, the bullet hits your ear. I didn't want to kill an innocent man. But you're safe now."

"I was safe before."

"I mean, he'll hear about this and not come after you again."

"Why would you think he would come after me he knows I don't keep anything of value at my home. I had great discussions with him and the others talking about how banks can be trusted. They took the other side of the argument I made it clear to all of them I never kept anything of value at home. They kept talking about their god damn Titan 1200-XR safes. If anyone is in danger and needs protection from this guy, it's Eugene Dohm or Randell Yang. The two of them were always bragging about how much they had and how they didn't trust banks."

Paul Tieden being a smart man was starting to put together that something went terribly wrong. "Why did you think he was coming for me?" Tieden asked.

Captain Colleen spoke up for the first time. "In his cabin behind a pile of logs, we found a crumpled-up piece of paper with your name on it, your address, today's date, and the time 12:45 PM. We wanted to catch him in the act."

220

Bobby stupidly threw in, "I don't know, maybe he was coming here because you could identify him." I wasn't doing that well with my lies. I didn't lie as well as I used to before recovery.

"There was a whole shipload of people who could identify him you think he was going to kill all of us? You know what I think. I think he set you up and you fell for it, and because of that, I've got a hole the size of a dime in my ear. You're probably good cops, but this time you fucked up big-time." They led him away and into the ambulance.

He had tricked us, the smart bastard, the piece of paper with the name Paul Tieden the date, and the time 12:45 pm written on it had been a ruse. The son of a bitch, Mr. Benjamin Thatch, had screwed us over big-time. And we fell for it because we were in such a rush to catch him. A rush he created.

That afternoon all hell broke loose down at the house. Chairs were being thrown up against the wall. The mood of the duty room was drearier than the surgical waiting room of a hospital when all cases that day were declared terminal. The question was, how terminal was this going to be?

After a week, the Chief of Police, Stan Maysack, called the four of us into his office. "Good day, my fuck-ups, good day. How are you today, Detective Colleen Donahue, and Officer Collins and Officer Hollander? We had all been demoted one rank. The good news is we weren't going to be fired." You could tell the Chief of Police was happy. The threat of Captain Colleen Donahue coming for his job was over. "And congratulations to Detective Sandy de Cotte, we're promoting you because of the excellent work you did to bring that crazy lady, Ms. Angela Allison, to justice. There was a bit of a gun battle, and she was wounded, but we got her. The Colorado Springs cops are quite happy, "And yes, the Colorado police actually shot a suspect instead of a citizen."

The only good news is Paul Tieden had decided not to sue the city. He wanted to get back to his normal life. He was tired of having all the parasitic news vans out in front of his house.

221

The gist of his letter absolving us of damages to his ear and house was kind. He said, "I guess the officers were trying to do the right thing. But in a rush to apprehend the suspect, mistakes were made. Daniel Ray (a Mr. Benjamin Thatch) did torture and kill the poor Yangs, Susan, and I are glad it wasn't us."

"That's putting it nicely. Mistakes were made."

The afternoon of the botched raid, it came through on the wire about the Yangs being tortured, murdered, and robbed. No mint was found. The police never let out that Ivana had been the one doing the torturing or the smile on her face when they found them. The Chief also never mentioned he gave the order to shoot.

Bobby had never felt so despondent except for maybe the first few days in treatment, and he had never felt like taking a drink like this since leaving treatment. It was like the only solution was for him to listen to that voice in his head and throw it all away. Bobby walked out of the police station. He walked down the block into a bar buying a bottle and then into the hotel. He would get a room. Drunks always love hotel rooms. There's no conscience in a hotel room, and they give you that wonderful sign that you can put on the door, "Do not disturb." He wanted to be left alone forever.

He got to the front desk. He was going to ask for a room but for some unknown reason, he asked the woman behind the counter to use her phone. He showed her his badge telling her it was official business.

He called his sponsor. It must've been a God thing because he rarely picked up, but he answered. "Spon--I'm down at the Kaylor Hotel. I've got a bottle."

Instead of sounding scared, alarmed, and panicked, his sponsor, knowing everything that had transpired in the last few weeks, said, "Well, that's an option, not a very good one, but it is an option. How about instead of getting that room. You walk out the door of the hotel stand by the curb, instead of crawling into it, and I'll be there in five minutes. We'll

222

either go have coffee, talk for as long as you need, or go to a meeting or both. Either way, I'm going to get in my car and come down there I'll pick you up outside by the curb, or I'll have the front desk tell me what room you're in, and I'll take you to detox."

Defiantly I said, "I could go to another hotel."

He just compassionately said, "Remember you called me or God had you call me, and I answer both types of calls. I can tell you things will get better, but they won't if you take that first drink, see you soon."

Five minutes later, Bobby's sponsor was driving up in front of the Kaylor Hotel. Bobby slid into the car. His sponsor leaned over, smelled his breath, "Good choice Bobby. What's your favorite coffee shop?"

"The little one on the ninth street, it's quiet in there. We can talk." I had left the full bottle on the curb. My sponsor stayed with me, Kay and Joey, for the next two days. It took me that long to regain my balance. I realized that even the people in, "Nobody Comes Back" section of town needed a good cop—one who's known good times and hard times but cared about them walking their streets. Maybe I could help a drunk or two.

At 10:30 AM, the morning of the fiasco. The man called Daniel Ray and was now to be known as Mr. Mark Martelly was sitting in his first-class seat on a plane bound for Ho Chi Minh City, waiting for the new 612 Airbus to take off. He thought, "If I were the cops, I would take me right before they close the plane doors." He looked at the passengers around, wondering if any were undercover. His hand was holding a plastic spike killing device like he had used on Angela's would-be rapist. He felt safe once the plane was off the ground, and the wheels were tucked away. He would be landing on foreign soil.

It was an uneventful flight. Mr. Martelly slept, something he hadn't done in days. Once he was on the ground in Ho Chi Minh City. He quickly went through customs with no incident, chuckling to himself, "I think

223

they're more worried more about things leaving the country than coming into it." For it was still quite easy to get an AK-47 in Vietnam.

Once he was out of the airport, he grabbed a cab and went straight to the hotel to relieve himself of his backside packages, which he cleaned off in the sink. He was so glad he had packaged them so well there were no tears or rips in any of the packages or his intestines. Not feeling tired yet, he sliced the packages open on the desk in his room. He sorted them by weight and grade. He was an expert gemologist even though he had no certificate. He put them in four velvet pouches and put them in the safe laid on the bed ordered room service had an excellent ribeye with fries and a salad. He then went into the bedroom, lay down, and slept for 12 hours.

The next day he set about looking for the two apartments. One was in the heart of the city where they would live, another one quickly accessible by car or subway, hopefully never to be used. But stocked well with weapons he would accumulate in the coming weeks. He went around to the five hotels picking up the packages of euros he had sent ahead. He was pleasantly surprised all five false bottom wood carved ornate boxes had arrived intact. He had not lost a single euro, their seed money for their new life. He rented the rooms on both sides of him, not for the extra space but for the room's safes in each of them to hold the euros. Now would come the task of finding safe places for their wealth.

The day came, and he when to the airport to meet his wife, he liked the word and would say it to himself often, "My wife, my wife." He was outside the immigration area standing there waiting for Angela. All the first-class passengers had passed through. And now, it appeared as if almost all the regular passengers had also passed through immigration. Things started to change inside of him again, but then he saw Angela or now to be known as Mrs. Janell Martelly. She had been helping an older woman steadying herself on Angela's arm. They were talking Vietnamese to each other, slowly walking along. Angela waved at me, and the older woman looked over at me and then patted Angela's arm. They were finishing some conversation.

The elderly woman pointed towards a younger woman. Angela smiled and handed the woman off to her daughter. The old woman bowed as did her daughter Angela bowed back but quickly ran, grabbed and hugged me, kissing me over and over. "Oh, my Daniel, I mean Mark, I love you," She whispered in his ear. "I'm still going to call you Daniel in private, and I'm never going to let you go. The older woman was so nice we got talking before the flight left. She needed the first-class seat more than I did, so we switched. She reminded me of my grandmother. And by the way, she thinks you're pretty cute."

My insides relaxed. "I'm glad you gave her your seat. I want to hear so much more about your grandmother and even the rest of your family. It's nice that we have a lifetime for that."

Angela got really close to me clearly, not wanting anyone to hear. "Mark." She smiled. "After an hour on the flight, I wish I hadn't given her my seat. My backside was so uncomfortable. I bet the cushy seats in the first-class section would've helped a lot. I didn't do as good of a job as you did putting things up my backside container." She giggled. "I still think calling it a container is so funny. Let's get to the hotel so I can get these things out of me put something I like much better in me if I can stay awake. I'm never going to leave you. I felt so scared on the plane what if you weren't here what I got off." I told her I had had the same fears. "I love you so much."

"Me too, honey me too now let's go to the hotel get you comfortable and get you some sleep." At the hotel, after everything was taken care of, she fell asleep locked in his arms. She was safe. Daniel loved looking out for her and that he could be with her for the rest of their life. We had made it.

After a couple of months, there was not even a hint of them being chased, so they returned to Heaven with an architect and made plans and drawing of the dream house that would be built overlooking the valley. They had no trouble buying the land, especially when they offered too much, to begin with.

Angela/Janell was true to her word; she never left his side. She was especially close seven months later when Daniel Ray was doing the last thing he needed to do to become Mark Martelly for good. He had plastic surgery changing his looks. After he healed, they would be moving to Heaven. Janell was by his side the entire time. He finally got to leave Daniel Ray and all the others behind. At least for now.